WILDSAM
FIELD GUIDES

D1601153

Sincere thanks to the Austin History Center, Bullock Texas State
History Museum, Dolph Briscoe Center for American History,
Texas Monthly, Jack Sanders and the Texas Playboys, Ben
Edgerton, John Spong, David Courtney, Stirling Kelso Neff,
Leigh Patterson, Liz Lambert and the Bunkhouse team, Steve
Wertheimer, Samantha Alviani, Carol and Byron Chin, Shelly
Colvin, Amy Pastre and Courtney Rowson; to Chris Bilheimer
and his wonderfully drawn city; to Robin Bruce and her love of
Texas and me; and to the Austin folks who kindly took me in the
summer of 2004 and showed me Mount Bonnell.

WILDSAM FIELD GUIDES™

A WILDSAM PRESS ORIGINAL,
MAY 2013

ISBN 978-0-578-12310-3

Art direction by Stitch Design Co.
Foldout map by Michael Newhouse

www.wildsam.com

⇒ CONTENTS ⇐

fig. 1

⟫ WELCOME ⟪

EDDIE WILSON'S VOICE IS A RUSTY BARREL, scratchy from 40 years of late nights, still strong enough to clear a room. He's sitting at Threadgill's, the legendary music tavern he now owns, where Janis Joplin got her start. And he's rattling off stories from back then with ease. The one about meeting Janis and her flipping him the bird. The one about Austin's first black disc jockey, Lavada Durst, aka Dr. Hepcat — "I wanted to be him so bad" — and how Lavada played Elvis before anyone else did. That one somehow reminds Eddie of his old club, the famous Armadillo World Headquarters, and the time Frank Zappa mopped up the floors and how Van Morrison loved the shrimp enchiladas.

Eddie is a master storyteller. His anecdotes flow into one another in an underground aquifer kind of way. His memories are fluid and bottomless. But, as he goes and goes, one story seems to swirl in a deeper pool than the rest. It's one about the Grateful Dead doing an impromptu show on a stormy Thanksgiving afternoon, and Doug Sahm leading the band, and how 1,500 people showed up, all whispering as they entered the hollow armory. Eddie lingers in that story.

"It started coming down pretty hard, so Doug and Jerry just played a full set of rain songs," Eddie says, his voice lilting upwards, as if still amazed. "That show was what inoculated the Armadillo from ever having to make sense."

If there's a red thread to Austin, this is it. The offbeat, the wide-open, the frontier disregard for boundaries. It's much more than weird. This sense of possibility feels a part of the limestone strata, cut long before taglines and tee shirts. Topographically, Austin is where East and West fuse. Politically, it's the blue dot in a blood-red state. Culturally, where barefoot and boots come together. As Liz Lambert says, "If you grow up in Texas and you're a little different, all roads lead to Austin."

That's why the Armadillo World Headquarters was more than a music hall. For a short time, it was the city at 100 proof — joyfully hellbent and unafraid of not making sense. No drought, no overcrowding, no MOPAC stand-still can touch that core element. Doug Sahm would call it the groove. Eddie Wilson would just call it Austin. -*TB*

ESSENTIALS

TRANSPORT

VINTAGE LIMO
Austin Classic Limo
512-517-0055
austinclassiclimo.com

....

LAKE RENTALS
Texas Rowing Center
1541 W Cesar Chavez
texasrowingcenter.com

....

BICYCLES
Mellow Johnny's
400 Nueces
mellowjohnnys.com

HOTELS

RETRO
Hotel San Jose
1316 S Congress Ave
sanjosehotel.com

....

ROCK AND ROLL
Hotel Saint Cecilia
112 Academy Dr
hotelsaintcecilia.com

....

NEW OPENING
South Congress Hotel
1603 S Congress Ave
southcongresshotel.com

PUBLICATIONS
Texas Monthly
Austin Chronicle
Texas Tribune
Tribeza

COFFEE
Flat Track
1619 E Cesar Chavez

....

Fleet
2427 Webberville Rd

....

Jo's Coffee
1300 S Congress

....

Patika
2159 S Lamar

CALENDAR
JAN   Tattoo Art Revival
FEB   Carnival Brasiliero
MAR   South by Southwest
APR   Eeyore's Birthday Party
MAY   World Championship
      Pun-Off
JUN   Juneteenth Celebrations
JUL   Deep Eddy Pool
      Splash Movies
AUG   Hot Sauce Festival
SEP   UT Football
OCT   Texas Book Festival
NOV   East Austin Studio Tour
DEC   Zilker Christmas Tree

BOOKS
➥ *Goodbye to a River* by
   John Graves
➥ *The Gay Place* by Billy
   Lee Brammer
➥ *Land of the
   Permanent Wave* by
   Bud Shrake

ONE DAY

Franklin Barbecue lunch
Barton Springs swim
C-Boy's Heart & Soul live music

....

WEEKEND

Lady Bird Lake run
Eastside dive bars
Veracruz All Natural tacos
Austin City Limits taping
Broken Spoke drop-in

FOODWAY

Breakfast Taco
The Tex-Mex answer to drive-
thru biscuits, this tinfoil tortilla
tradition satisfies everyone,
from late-rising slackers to pre-
dawn construction crews.

EMERGENCY

Heart Hospital of Austin
3801 N Lamar, 512-407-7000

RADIO

KGSR 93.3
KUTX 98.9

RECORD COLLECTION

Willie Nelson	*Shotgun Willie*
Butthole Surfers	*Electriclarryland*
Alejandro Escovedo	*Gravity*
Jerry Jeff Walker	*Viva Terlingua*
Patty Griffin	*1,000 Kisses*
Doug Sahm & The Tex-Mex Trip	*Groover's Paradise*
Stevie Ray Vaughan & Double Trouble	*Texas Flood*
Gary Clark Jr.	*Blak and Blu*
Christopher Cross	*Christopher Cross*
Explosions in the Sky	*The Earth Is Not A Cold Dead Place*
Flatlanders	*Live at the One Knite*
Sarah Jarosz	*Follow Me Down*
Spoon	*Ga Ga Ga Ga Ga*

ESSENTIALS

STATISTICS

2,591	Number of tech companies in Austin
5.6%	2012 Austin's unemployment rate
27%	Drop in Central East Austin's black population since 2000
40%	Rise in white population over same period
1	Best Cities for Young Adults, *Forbes*
91.6	Avg temp in Aug 2011, 10 degrees higher than 1855

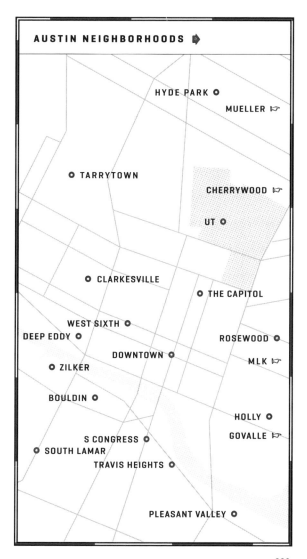

AUSTIN NEIGHBORHOODS ➡

HYDE PARK ○

MUELLER ☞

○ TARRYTOWN

CHERRYWOOD ☞

UT ○

○ CLARKESVILLE

○ THE CAPITOL

WEST SIXTH ○

DEEP EDDY ○

ROSEWOOD ○

DOWNTOWN ○

MLK ☞

○ ZILKER

BOULDIN ○

HOLLY ○

GOVALLE ☞

S CONGRESS ○

○ SOUTH LAMAR

TRAVIS HEIGHTS ○

PLEASANT VALLEY ○

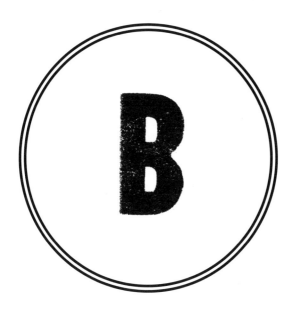

BEST

*A curated list of citywide favorites including burgers,
biergartens, cycling routes, rodeos, moviehouses, river floats,
fiction writing, taxidermy and more*

≫ FOOD & DRINK ≪

CORNER CAFE
Launderette
2115 Holly St
East Austin
launderetteaustin.com
Lovingly transformed laundry now a hopping café-bar-patio with American fare.

....

WOOD GRILLED
Fresas
1703 S First
Bouldin Creek
fresaschicken.com
Charry yardbird with a citrusy kick or Yucatan spice, and A+ frozen margaritas.

....

HAMBURGER
Hut's
807 W 6th St
Downtown
512-472-0693
No-fuss longhorn burgers slathered

with mayo like grandpa taught you.

....

BBQ
Micklethwait
Craft Meats
1309 Rosewood Ave
East Austin
craftmeatsaustin.com
Serving peppery brisket and juicy beef ribs from a trailer. Fifteen minute wait.

....

INSTITUTION
Fonda San Miguel
2330 W. North Loop
North Loop
fondasanmiguel.com
Feels like a grand hacienda that serves the best mole this side of Mexico.

....

BRASSERIE
Justine's
4710 E 5th St

East Austin
justines1937.com
Two glasses in, you'll swear you've traveled to an offbeat Parisian 'hood.

....

GULF SEAFOOD
Quality Seafood
5621 Airport Blvd
North Loop
512-454-5827
That salty, unassuming, 75-year-old fisherman's haunt that locals swear by.

....

SUSHI
Uchi
801 S Lamar
Bouldin
uchiaustin.com
Beard-winning Tyson Cole defied the landlocked logic and built a new icon.

SODA FOUNTAIN

Nau's Enfield Drugs

115 West Lynn St
Enfield
nausdrug.com

Lunch counter relic
with thick milk-
shakes and patty
melts, a la 1950.

....

BREAKFAST TACO

Veracruz All Natural

1704 E Cesar Chavez
Holly
512-981-1760

Their morning
migas taco wins
the biggest debate
in the city.

....

FINE DINING

Jeffrey's

1204 W Lynn St
Clarksville
jeffreysofaustin.com

A revamped institu-
tion with a roving
martini cart and
some serious steaks.

....

VIETNAMESE

Elizabeth Street Café

1501 S First
Bouldin
elisabethstreetcafe.com

The bright Viet-
namese bakery
dishes out inspired
báhn mì and pho.

KOLACHE

Hruska's Store

Hwy 71, Southeast
Ellinger

Czech pastry pur-
ists drive 71 miles
for this bready
sausage snack.

....

BIERGARTEN

Easy Tiger

709 E 6th St
Downtown
easytigeraustin.com

Part bread bakery,
part beerman's
hang — with creek-
side ping pong.

....

ICE CREAM

Lick

2032 S Lamar
South Austin
ilikelick.com

Goat cheese, sea
salt caramel,
roasted beets —
worth every cold
headache.

....

MARGARITA

La Condesa

400 W 2nd St
Downtown
lacondesaaustin.com

Silver lightning cut
with Citronge, wrung
limes and a cactus-
lemongrass kick.

PATIO

Contigo

2027 Anchor Ln
Mueller
contigoaustin.com

Ranch-inspired
spot proves the
best rooms in Texas
aren't found inside.

....

COCKTAILS

Small Victory

108 E 7th St
Downtown
smallvictory.bar

Sliver of a bar wins
the night. Try the
Rosita, like a Negroni
but with tequila.

....

PUB

The Draught House

4112 Medical Pkwy
Rosedale
draughthouse.com

The woody brewhaus
welcomes tailgaters
and passes out free
brats on Saturdays.

....

LATE NIGHT

24 Diner

600 N Lamar
West Austin
24diner.com

Cure the midnight
blues with the
chef's sweet onion
gravy meatloaf.

≫ SHOPPING ≪

BOOKS
BookPeople
603 N Lamar
Clarksville
bookpeople.com
Four-story hub that keeps Austin smart, open everyday but Thanksgiving.
....

RECORDS
Waterloo
600A N Lamar
Clarksville
waterloorecords.com
Staff is the best kind of picky at this unofficial music museum of the city.
....

RANCH
Callahans
501 Bastrop Hwy
Montopolis
callahansgeneral-store.com
Need some sweet feed? A new scythe handle? How's about a goat?
....

TREASURES
Bell and Bird
1206 W 38th St
Hyde Park
bellandbird.com
Heirloom jewelry shop owners search old-world estates far and wide.
....

HOME GOODS
Kettle and Brine
908 W 12th St
Clarksville
kettleandbrine.com
Homage to finer details of everyday life, via curated tabletop and pantry items.
....

CACTI
East Austin Succulents
801 Tillery St
East Austin
eastaustinsucculents.com
Neighborhood plant place with thousands of prickly specimens in a funky greenhouse.
....

MEN'S SHOP
Stag
1423 S Congress
South Congress
stagaustin.com
For fashionable fellas who dig Made-in-America heritage brands.
....

WOMEN'S SHOP
By George
524 N Lamar
Clarksville
bygeorgeaustin.com
Lucky top ten boutique that carries the tough-to-find labels.

BOOTS

Helm Boots
1200 E 11th St
East Austin
helmboots.com
Handmade, hard-
working boots with
all the fancy-stitch
details.

....

OUTDOOR APPAREL

Howler Brothers
1010 W Lynn St
Clarksville
howlerbros.com
Casual clothes that
channel days of
surfing and fly fish-
ing adventures.

....

PEACHES

Vogel Orchards
12862 U.S. 290
Stonewall
830-644-2404

Stop at the open-air
stand, then Sunday-
drive the gorgeous
Gellerman Lane.

....

CHEESE

Antonelli's
4220 Duval St
Hyde Park
antonellischeese.com
Husband-wife
cheesemongers in a
super-friendly, try-
before-you-buy shop.

TEQUILA

Wiggy's
1130 W 6th St
Clarksville
512-474-9463
Creaky-floor spirits
cave with smart
selection of the
strong stuff.

....

HOMEBREW

Austin Homebrew
Supply
9129 Metric Blvd
North Burnet
austinhomebrew.com
Spreading the hoppy
gospel since 1991,
started Rogness
Brewery in 2012.

....

MEXICAN GROCERY

La Michoacana
1917 E 7th St
East Austin
lamichoacanameat-
market.com
Meat market, pan-
deria, taqueria — as
close to Guadalajara
as you can get.

....

BICYCLES

Mellow Johnny's
400 Nueces St
Downtown
mellowjohnnys.com
Pro-service, showers
for commuters,

Juan Pelota Café.

....

MOTORCYCLES

Revival Cycles
1603 S Congress
Govalle
revivalcycles.com
Vintage bikes tin-
kered on by moto
aficionados.

....

LOCAL DESIGNER

Esby
1601 S First St
Bouldin Creek
esbyapparel.com
Stephanie Beard's
seasonal lines are as
comfy as they are cool.

....

MODERN GIFT

Take Heart
1111 E 11th St
East Austin
takeheartshop.com
Cozy gift shop that
carries lovingly se-
lected objects from
small brands.

....

SPORTSWEAR

Outdoor Voices
606 Blanco St
WEST SIXTH
outdoorvoices.com
Super stylish
workout gear for
yoga, lake runs, and
long mornings.

≫ ACTION ≪

DANCEHALL

Gruene Hall

New Braunfels
gruenehall.com

Circa 1878, the
clapboard dancehall
is legendary among
Texas troubadours.

....

RACING

Circuit of the
Americas

9201 Circuit of the
Americas Blvd
circuitoftheamericas.com

First US track built
for Formula 1,
held 117,000 for
first race in 2012.

....

CYCLING ROUTE

New Dam Loop

923 Barton Springs Rd
austintricyclist.com

Fifty-five miler
follows part of a
classic hills route,

diverts for a mellow
descent home.

....

MUSIC FESTIVAL

Fun Fun Fun Fest

funfunfunfest.com
November

Genre-based festival
for lesser-known art-
ists in hip-hop, punk,
indie rock.

....

RIVER FLOAT

Comal River

250 Meusebach
New Braunfels
comalrivertubing.com

Lazy summer flotil-
las in the gin-clear
Guadalupe tributary.

....

CINEMA

Violet Crown

434 W 2nd St
Downtown
violetcrowncinema.com

Modern arthouse

space with reserved
stadium seating and
cut-short previews.

....

CELEBRATION

Eeyore's birthday

Pease Park

Austin's classic
shindig honoring
Pooh's donkey pal
every April.

....

COMEDY

Master Pancake

Drafthouse.com

The Alamo folks
serve beer, play
bad movies, and
let the comedians
do the rest.

....

DUDE RANCH

Mayan Ranch

Bandera
mayanranch.com

Family spread in the
Hill Country is home

to everyone's favorite, Kowgirl Kel.

....

PUBLIC ART
Frank
4th and Colorado
Stepped-up hotdog-gery lends its outer brick wall to local artists quarterly.

....

ANTIQUES
Round Top
Fayette County
roundtopantiques.com
Two weekends a year this Central Texas mapdot swarms with America's best pickers.

....

COUNTRY DRIVE
Ranch Road 165
From 290 to Blanco
Getting lost in the westward hills means finding Texas' answer to Tuscany.

....

LAVENDER
Hill Country Lavender
Blanco
830-833-2860
hillcountrylavender.com

Cut your own from 2,500 plants on this hilly, per-fumed spread, the state's first.

....

URBAN FARM
Boggy Creek Farm
3414 Lyons Rd
boggycreekfarm.com
Established in 1992, ahead of the contemporary push for slow and local.

....

WAKEBOARDING
Freeride Wakeboard School
512-796-0832
freeridewake.com
Elite lessons from world champ Billy Garcia for newbies or shredders.

....

LITERATURE
Ransom Center
21st and Quadalupe
The Drag
Hrc.utexas.edu
The bibliophile's Smithsonian archives America's canon of letters.

[LONG] ROADTRIP
Marfa
Far West
visitmarfa.com
It's 441 miles to Judd's crossroads of Chihuahuan desert and modern art.

....

GEOLOGICAL WONDER
Enchanted Rock
16710 Ranch Rd 965
Fredericksburg
Natives believed the moonish pink monadnock to be a holy portal.

....

SXSW SECRET
Central Presbyterian Church
200 E 8th St
Downtown
Put the beer down, catch your breath, settle into a pew for a set or two.

....

ARCADE
Arcade UFO
3101 Speedway
Hyde Park
arcadeufo.com
Japanese-style hub for gamers.

≫ EXPERTISE ≪

RUNNING
Steve Sisson
Rogue Running
410 Pressler St
roguerunning.com
Former assistant
track coach at UT,
5000m record
holder for ten years.
....

ARCHITECT
Kevin Alter
Alter Studio
alterstudio.net
Studio has won over
60 design awards for
its social-minded
modern shelter
design.
....

TORTILLA MAKER
Sonia Vasquez-Grizzle
Margarita's
Gourmet Tortillas
margaritastortilla-
factory.com
Started in 1997

with $5k, now sells
across Austin and
in Whole Foods
throughout Texas.
....

BODY SHOP
Dave's Perfection
1804 S 1st St
512-444-5919
Definitely the place
for classic cars, now
run by Continental
Club owner.
....

ARTIST-DESIGNER
Alyson Fox
alysonfox.com
Textile designer
and cool-stuff maker
has collaborated
with West Elm.
....

FICTION
Oscar Casares
oscarcasares.com
Professor and
noted author of

Brownsville border
stories and a novel,
Amigoland.
....

GUITAR REPAIR
South Austin Music
1402 S. Lamar
southaustinmusic.com
Pedal, amp and
guitar repair by trusty
technicians next door
to Saxon Pub.
....

CASTING
Beth Sepko
bethsepkocasting.com
Respected local
insider who's worked
with Richard
Linklater, Robert
Rodriguez, *Friday*
Night Lights.
....

RESTAURANTEUR
Larry McGuire
mcguiremoorman.com
Since Lambert's,

he's partnered to open Perla's, Elizabeth Street, Clark's Oyster Bar and a reinvented Jeffrey's.

....

MUSIC JOURNALIST
Margaret Moser
austinchronicle.com
Pioneer punk-rock columnist at the *Austin Chronicle,* central player in Austin Music Awards.

....

TAXIDERMY
Martinez Brothers
2057 S. Lamar
martinezbrothers.net
Family has been mounting white tail deer, javalina and grizzlies since 1959.

....

POLITICO
Ross Ramsey
texastribune.com
Managing Editor of *Tribune,* go-to source behind *Texas Weekly* political newsletter since 1998.

....

SANDLOT BASEBALL
The Texas Playboys
texasplayboys-baseball.com

Motley lineup of writers and artists play spirited pickups, founded by Jack Sanders in 2006.

....

BRAND DESIGN
LAND
East Austin
workbyland.com
The eastside duo behind iconographic work for Folk Fibers, Easy Tiger, Mollyjogger and Deus Ex Machina.

....

EQUINE VET
Nick Moore
mooredvm.com
Mobile clinic based out of Georgetown, specializes in horse dentistry and lameness.

....

JAZZ
Esperanza Spalding
esperanzaspalding.com
First jazz artist to win Best New Artist Grammy, soulful singer and bass virtuosa lives half the year in Austin.

SOUND ENGINEER
Jim Eno
Founding member of Spoon, produced records for Black Joe Lewis, Alejandro Escovedo and Heartless Bastards.

....

COACH
Hank Carter
laketravisfootball.com
Powerhouse Cavaliers program has five straight titles, bruising defense and 77-3 record.

....

BAT EXPERTS
Bat Conservation International
batcon.org
In Austin since 1986, world leaders in bat conservation, team of fearless cave explorers.

....

JEWELRY MAKER
Margot Wolf
margotwolf.com
Uses copper, silver and bronze, casts natural specimens like flower buds and shells, sells at By George.

ALMANAC

*A deep dive into the cultural heritage of Austin
through timelines, how-tos, newspaper clippings, lineups,
letters, poems and historical hearsay*

SOUTH BY SOUTHWEST

1987 .... 172 acts including Rev. Horton Heat and Dash Dip Rock
1988 .... "SXSW SUX" tee-shirts printed by local band
1989 .... Flock of Seagulls refuses to share bill
1990 .... Over 1,500 acts apply for 424 spots
1991 .... Arson outside SXSW offices by disgruntled fans
1992 .... Michelle Shocked's controversial address on race
1993 .... Relative-unknown Marilyn Manson speaks on panel
1994 .... Johnny Cash keynote and solo set at Emo's
1995 .... Three-part SXSW setup made official
1996 .... Over 860 acts perform
1997 .... Flaming Lips' 30-cars-30-cassettes symphony
1998 .... Sonic Youth, Queens of the Stone Age, the Donnas
1999 .... Tom Waits vows never to play Texas again
2000 .... Invasion of Swedish bands
2001 .... Ike Turner is one of 1,159 acts
2002 .... Norah Jones plays upstairs at an Indian restaurant
2003 .... 7,000 war protestors fill streets near Capitol
2004 .... Little Richard keynote speech
2005 .... MTV Real World filming in Austin
2006 .... Arctic Monkeys, Wikipedia founder draw crowds
2007 .... Twitter blows up
2008 .... Bon Iver, Lady GaGa, and Lou Reed
2009 .... Foursquare and *The Hurt Locker*
2010 .... Bill Murray bartends at Shangri-La
2011 .... 20,000 Interactive attendees
2012 .... Springsteen's keynote: "Dylan gave us the words"
2013 .... Space travel talk and Grumpy Cat
2014 .... "Pi in the sky" spelled out with sky-writing

MOONTOWERS

Since 1895, residents of Austin have lived dusk-to-dawn under the soft moonglow of 150-foot iron towers, topped each with six mercury-vapor lamps powerful enough to let a man read his wristwatch 1,000 yards away. Rumors attribute the moontower project to the unsolved servant girl murders ten years prior, but no direct connection exists on record.

CIVIL WAR

GRAND WAR BARBECUE!!!
Tri-Weekly State Gazette
November 6, 1863_

The Sons of the South, of Camp Confederacy, No. 1, send greeting to their brethren of the various sister encampments of Texas, and cordially invite them to a Grand War Barbecue, to be given by the order near this city on the second Thursday of next month. A like earnest welcome is extended to the citizens of Travis and surrounding counties, also, to all, however remote, who may find it convenient to be present. Especially are the mothers, wives, sisters and daughters of the valiant soldiery of Texas, embraced within this invitation; most respectfully and warmly are they solicited to honor the occasion with their presence. Distinguished speakers will be in attendance to rehearse the story of our country's wrongs, recount the valorous achievements of brave southrons on the battle fields.

THE RANGER'S PRAYER

_Written by Pierre Bernard Hill, a former Texas Ranger Chaplain
and Poet Laureate of Texas from 1955-57._

O God, Whose end is justice,
Whose strength is all our stay,
Be near and bless my mission
As I go forth today.
Let wisdom guide my actions,
Let courage fill my heart
And help me, Lord, in
   every hour
To do a Ranger's part.
Protect when danger threatens,
Sustain when trails are rough;
Help me to keep my
   standard high

And smile at each rebuff.
When night comes down
   upon me,
I pray thee, Lord, be nigh,
Whether on lonely scout,
   or camped,
Under the Texas sky.
Keep me, O God, in life
And when my days shall end,
Forgive my sins and
   take me in,
For Jesus' sake, Amen.

DRIPPING SPRINGS REUNION

March 17-19, 1972

It was perhaps the most important weekend in the history of Austin. Even though it was a complete flop. Promoters organized the "Dripping Springs Reunion" as an Opry-in-Texas kind of gig, with Nashville pillars like Hank Snow, Earl Scruggs, and Tom T. Hall getting top billing. They held it in the middle of a dusty field in the nothing-town of Dripping Springs, a few miles outside Austin, and hyped it as a country music Woodstock, predicting upwards of 200,000 people. On Friday, 700 folks showed. Even the 10,000 that came out on Sunday felt like a bust. But, the shindig turned out to be perhaps the biggest turning point in Willie Nelson's career, when Stetson ranchers and long-haired hippies stood side-by-side for the birth of Outlaw Country. Three months later, Willie played the famous Zilker Park McGovern Rally. Soon after that, his first Armadillo World Headquarters show. Something new was born, and off the Redheaded Stranger went.

FRIDAY	SATURDAY	SUNDAY
Bluegrass Festival	Charlie Walker	Merle Haggard
Bill Monroe	Hank Snow	Tom T. Hall
Earl Scruggs	Sonny James	Willie Nelson
Buck Owens	Roger Miller	Waylon Jennings
Roy Acuff	Tex Ritter	Loretta Lynn
		Kris Kristofferson

CEDAR CHOPPERS

Often derided for daywandering, and a mountaineer's reek, cedar choppers were for several decades quite ubiquitous in Austin and nearby counties. Cousins to roughnecks and hillbillies, cedar choppers were extraordinary axe-handlers. They dealt in cash and drove wobbly pickups. And as barbed wire made cedar posts an essential, the roaming laborers scrubbed evergreen hills clear of Ashe juniper and trucked their loots to ranchers. As remembered, snakes and runaway brakes were always archenemies. But freedom — or laziness, depending on your source — was the great reward.

Common Name	*Description of Bloom… Date*
Texas Bluebonnet	*violet-blue roadside epiphanies… Mar-May*
Indian Blanket	*radiant orange and yellow pinwheels… May-Sep*
Purple Coneflower	*pinkish-purple with red-orange center… June-Oct*
Tickseed	*single bright yellow crowns… May-July*
Missouri Primrose	*cup-shaped canary yellow perennials… May-Sep*
Lemon Mint	*deep lavender colored whorls… May-Aug*
Drummond Phlox	*ruby red, upright clusters… Apr-June*
Tall Poppy Mallow	*purply petals close every evening… Mar-Aug*
Clasping Coneflower	*dropping yellow petals, black cone head… June-Sep*
Maximilian Sunflower	*rich yellow flowers craved by deer, cattle… July-Oct*
Gloriosa Daisy	*sunflower cousin, purple-brown center… June-Aug*
Standing Cypress	*bright red starfish-shaped flowers… June-Aug*
Showy Primrose	*colonies of soft pinks open for single day… Mar-July*
Mexican Hat	*crimson, yellow-flecked sombreros… June-Sep*
Texas Paintbrush	*white flower swaddled in red bracts… Mar-May*
Scarlet Sage	*butterflies flutter at the neon red… Apr-Frost*
Greenthread	*daisy-like with thin leaves… Mar-June*
Wine Cup	*cabernet color, vine-like across ground… Feb-July*
Bachelor's Button	*intensely blue ring of florets… Mar-May*
Mealy Blue Sage	*native Texan, undeterred by drought… Mar-Nov*
Engelmann Daisy	*drought-tolerant yellow flowers… Mar-July*
Greenthread	*skinny stem, rich mustard-tint petals… May-July*
Western Bitterweed	*sunflower cousin turns pastures yellow… Apr-June*
Golden-Wave Coreopsis	*golden petals with inner maroon rim… April-July*

UNIVERSITY OF TEXAS FOOTBALL

Unanimous All Americans

Year	Player	POS
1950	Bud McFadin	*Guard*
1961	James Saxton	*Running Back*
1963	Scott Appleton	*Tackle*
1971	Jerry Sisemore	*Offensive Tackle*
1972	Jerry Sisemore	*Offensive Tackle*
1973	Bill Wyman	*Center*
1977	Brad Shearer	*Defensive Tackle*
1977	Earl Campbell	*Running Back*
1978	Johnnie Johnson	*Defensive Back*
1979	Johnnie Johnson	*Defensive Back*
1979	Steve McMichael	*Defensive Tackle*
1981	Kenneth Sims	*Defensive Tackle*
1984	Jerry Gray	*Defensive Back*
1997	Ricky Williams	*Running Back*
1998	Ricky Williams	*Running Back*
2001	Quentin Jammer	*Cornerback*
2004	Derrick Johnson	*Linebacker*
2005	Jonathan Saxton	*Offensive Tackle*
2005	Michael Huff	*Corner Back*
2006	Justin Blalock	*Guard*
2008	Brian Orakpo	*Defensive End*
2009	Colt McCoy	*Quarterback*

BATS

Every summer close to 750,000 Mexican free-tailed bats — the great majority of which are pregnant females — make a home in the beams of the Ann W. Richards Congress Avenue Bridge. At dusk, the bats flash from their concrete grotto to feed on tens of thousands of moths and insects, an essential service to Texas farmers. The evening ritual draws watchers on both sides of Lady Bird Lake well into October, when most of the colony, now doubled in population, dart through the night back to Mexico.

MAIL RIDER

Daily Bulletin
December 28, 1841

A party of gentlemen left town Sunday evening to search for the missing mail-rider from San Antonio. They returned yesterday, having found the body of the unfortunate man about twelve miles from here, upon the Gonzales road. He had been killed by the Indians and scalped. His body when found had been mutilated by the wolves. The mail was not found, and the letters directed to civilized people will have strange delivery. We suppose they will be curiously examined in some gorge of the mountains above us, but will probably be Sybilline leaves to their possessors.

LYNDON B. JOHNSON

The answer was waiting for me in the land where I was born.

It was once barren land. The angular hills were covered with scrub cedar and a few live oaks. Little would grow in the harsh caliche soil. And each spring the Pedernales River would flood the valley.

But men came and worked and endured and built.

Today that country is abundant with fruit, cattle, goats and sheep. There are pleasant homes, and lakes, and the floods are gone.

Why did men come to that once forbidden land?

Well, they were restless, of course, and had to be moving on. But there was more than that. There was a dream — a dream of a place where a free man could build for himself, and raise his children to a better life — a dream of a continent to be conquered, a world to be won, a nation to be made.

Remembering this, I knew the answer.

President Lyndon B. Johnson
State of the Union address, 1965

JANIS JOPLIN

"SHE DARES TO BE DIFFERENT"
The Daily Texan
July 27, 1962

She goes barefooted when she feels like it, wears Levi's to class because they're more comfortable, and carries her Autoharp with her everywhere she goes so that in cause she gets the urge to break into song it will be handy.

Her name is Janis Joplin and she looks like the type of girl a square [her more descriptive term—a "leadbelly,"] would call a "beatnik."

"Jivey" is what Janis calls herself, not "beat." She leads a life that is enviously unrestrained. She doesn't bother to have her hair set every week, or to wear the latest feminine fashion fads, and when she feels like singing, she sings in a vibrant alto voice.

Since she has never had a music lesson and cannot read notes, her voice is untrained. But this lack seems to be an asset rather than a liability, for Janis sings with a certain sponta-

neity and gusto that cultivated voices sometimes find difficult to capture. She is at her best with folk songs, to which she gives an earthy, twangy rendition.

Janis' current ambition is to be a folksinger, though she really prefers blues. She has performed at the Gas House in Venice, Calif., and in Port Arthur, her hometown. But she really began to think seriously about singing when she came to the University, this year as a freshman majoring in art.

She says that people in Austin are definitely more hip on folk music than the colds in others cities she has visited. In fact, it was here that a friend persuaded her to take up the Autoharp.

Patricia Sharpe wrote this piece while a student at UT. She's an executive editor at Texas Monthly.

THE FLOOD

Apr 11, 1900.

My Dear Uncle,

Well I suppose you have done heard of the great calamity that has befell Austin by the washing away of the great granite dam across the Colorado River and Power House. Also the city is now without power lights and water — the dam and power house cost two million dollars. The river was higher than it had ever bin before the great wave came that washed away the dam. It was an awful sight. A good many people were drowned and several houses were washed away. They say it was a mericle that more was not drowned. I never want to experience another such a time. Couriers were sent all over the low flats of the city for the people all to flee for their lives to the hills. You never saw such a stampede — men, women and children all going as fast as they could and crying and praying. There was not a soul left in the flats. Everyone left there houses open and never took time to get a thing. Almost all the ladies and children were bare headed...when we reached a higher part of the city I stood and saw three houses go down the river.

Mary Gordon, 1401 Willow St.

SILICON HILLS

Tech companies working in Austin

3M Corporation

Advanced Micro Devices

Apple

Applied Materials

Bazaarvoice

BMC Software

Cirrus Logic

Cisco

Convio

CSC Financial Services

Dell

eBay

Freescale Semiconductor

Hewlett-Packard

HomeAway

IBM Corp.

Intel Corp.

LifeSize

National Instruments

Overwatch

Pervasive

Polycom

Samsung Austin Semiconductor

Spansion

Tokyo Electron

VMWare

Whaleshark Media

SERIAL KILLER

"TWO WOMEN DRAGGED FROM THEIR BEDS, MALTREATED, AND MURDERED"

New York Times
December 25, 1885

AUSTIN, Texas — Two brutal murders were committed in the heart of the city last night, almost within the sight of the great Capitol. It is just a year ago since a series of most mysterious outrages and assassinations was begun against the servant women of Austin. Within this year 13 colored women are known to have been outraged, seven of whom were afterward brutally murdered. Eight white women were attacked on the street or in rooms, four outraged, and three murdered. Nearly every one of these crimes bore evidence of having been perpetrated by the same ruffians, and the entire Police Department has been mystified. Over 400 arrests have been made and some of the suspected negroes were subjected to very severe examinations, but they would confess nothing. Northern detectives have been employed for the past six months to ferret out the criminals. Many people believe the murders were committed by some cunning madman, who is insane on the subject of killing women. Following out this theory, nearly every man in the city, black and white, known to have idiosycracies of any kind have been watched by the detectives, but without avail.

...A bloody trail led to the door and thence out the front door. Seizing a lamp Hancock followed the trail in his night clothes. It led around the house into the back yard, where near the rear of the lot, he found his wife, lying in a pool of blood and moaning faintly. She had received two terrible cuts across the head with an axe. One blow severed the ear and cut into the cheek bone; the other blow was between the ear and eye, and fractured the skull. Although alive this evening, the doctors give no positive hope of her recovering consciousness. She was a beautiful woman, about 40 years of age...

At nearly the same hour, in another part of the city, a dozen squares away, Ella Phillips, was missing, her pillow bloody and the covers thrown back. Search for the missing wife was instituted, and a bloody trail was found leading...into another back yard to some out buildings. The woman's body lay in a pool of blood. She had been dead perhaps half an hour, struck in the forehead with the butt end of an axe. The skull was broken. She had been outraged and most brutally maltreated. [Mr.] Phillips shows signs of consciousness, and keeps calling for his wife. The physicians have no hope for his recovery.

This makes three victims in one night. At 1 o'clock this morning the entire population is in the streets, excitedly conversing...If the fiends are apprehended, the citizens are determined that they shall be hanged in the sight of the Capitol. Half a dozen negroes were arrested to-night on mere suspicion.

MONIKERS

WATERLOO The legend is that after future Texas Republic president, Mirabeau Lamar, shot a giant buffalo near today's Eighth and Congress, he founded Waterloo, a small riverside village that would later be chosen as the capitol.

CITY OF THE VIOLET CROWN Texas newspaper journalist William Brann gave Austin her most lovely sobriquet in 1891, when he wrote of the city's "violet crown bathed in the radiance of the morning" — an ode that real estate developers still weave in to their trade.

KEEP AUSTIN WEIRD Coined by research librarian Red Wassenich, the catchy uproar for indie expression stuck, enough so to spook Borders from moving in next to BookPeople. The trademarked phrase is now worth millions, oddly enough.

TEXAS MONTHLY

*Since 1973, the National Magazine of Texas has cultivated
new journalistic chops with a Lone Star-meets-*Life *bent.
Here, eleven greatest hits.*

LEROY'S REVENGE
Ringside as two dogs— father
and son— fight to the death
Gary Cartwright, Aug 1975

CANDY
Stripper Candy Barr, the
forbidden fruit of Dallas, looks
back on her life
Gary Cartwright, Dec 1976

THE PETRIFIED FOREST*
Life in deep East Texas, where
lumber is king and the Civil
War was yesterday
Richard West, April 1978

THE MAN IN THE BLACK
HAT, I &II*
The mysterious ways of Clinton
Manges' South Texas empire
Paul Burka, June-July 1984

THE CHEERLEADER
MURDER PLOT
A cheerleader's mother does
the unthinkable
Mimi Swartz, May 1991

MANHUNT AT
MENARD CREEK
Chasing a thief for two
days in the Big Thicket
Robert Draper, Oct 1993

LANCE ARMSTRONG HAS
SOMETHING TO GET OFF
HIS CHEST
How much scrutiny can the
two-time Tour de France
winner stand?
Michael Hall, July 2001

STILL LIFE*
The story of a boy paralyzed
during a high school
football game
Skip Hollandsworth, May 2009

OF MEAT AND MEN
Two pitmasters, their devoted
fans, and some of the best
brisket you'll ever eat
Katy Vine, Feb 2012

THAT 70'S SHOW
Forty years ago, the birth
of outlaw country changed
music forever
John Spong, April 2012

INNOCENT MAN, I & II*
The story of Michael Morton
and one of the most profound
miscarriages of justice in
Texas history
Pamela Colloff, Nov-Dec 2012

*National Magazine Award winner

WHOLE FOODS HISTORY

THE ARMADILLO

The armadillo. Begrudged, beloved, misunderstood. Relatively unchanged in 50 million years, the armadillo has always been a survivor [unless found underneath a speeding F-150, in which case the sensitive souls instinctively launch themselves into the deadly undercarriage]. Their leathery armored shells give them the appearance of gladiator possoms, but no vicious bones can be found in their slothy bodies. Here's the big truth: Armadillos are a kind bunch. They are gentle prowlers, sidestepping confrontation, openly sharing their burrows with rabbits and skunks. They eat up termites. Root out scorpions. And their females live half their lives pregnant, giving birth to identical quadruplets nearly always. Yet the rap in Texas has mostly been negative — strewn carcasses, crop killers, yucky little beasts. Except in Austin. Here, the Texas armadillo is the offbeat doppelgänger to the Texas Longhorn. Bronzed onto belt buckles, flown on flags, mascot for punk rock. King of weird.

DEATH ROW

Since 1982, there have been 496 executions in the state of Texas,
accounting for nearly a third of the total performed in the U.S.
Just before lethal injection begins, the warden asks each inmate for
any final words. Here, a sampling from the last three decades.

Ramon Torres Hernandez **11/14/12**
Can you hear me? Did I ever tell you, you have dad's eyes? I've noticed that in the last couple of days.

....

Lee Taylor **6/16/11**
Prison is a bad place. I am sorry that I killed him. There are 300 people on Death Row, and everyone is not a monster.

....

Robert Lee Thompson **11/19/09**
Yes, I bear witness that there is no God, but Allah. From Allah we came and from Allah we will return. We all have to walk this path. Assalamu Alaikum. Allah is the forgiver. Go ahead Warden.

....

Larry Davis **7/31/08**
Blessed are they that mourn, for they shall be comforted. It is finished.

....

Vincent Gutierrez **3/28/07**
My brother, where's my stunt double when you need one?

....

Donell Jackson **11/1/06**
To my family, first and foremost, I love you all. The calmness that I was telling you about, I still

have it. I'm alright. Make sure momma knows, a right.

....

Douglas Roberts **4/20/05**
Before I leave, I want to tell you all. When I die, bury me deep, lay two speakers at my feet, put some headphones on my head and rock and roll me when I'm dead. That's all Warden.

....

Cameron Todd Willingham **2/17/04**
I am an innocent man, convicted of a crime I did not commit. I have been persecuted for 12 years for something I did not do. From God's dust I came and to dust I will return, so the earth shall become my throne. I gotta go road dog.

....

Michael Moore **1/9/02**
I am sorry. If I could think of a word in the vocabulary stronger, you need to hear something stronger, you deserve it. I'm sorry.

....

Jermarr Arnold **1/16/02**
I cannot explain and can't give you answers. I can give you one thing,

and I'm going to give that today.

....

Robert Carter   **5/31/00**
It was me and me alone. Anthony Graves had nothing to do with it. I lied on him in court. Anthony Graves don't even know anything about it.

....

David Hicks   **1/20/00**
Hey, how y'all doing out there? I done lost my voice. Y'all be strong now, alright? I love you, Gloria, always baby. That's all I got to say. Hey, don't y'all worry about me, okay?

....

John Lamb   **11/17/99**
I'm sorry, I wish I could bring them back. I'm done, let's do it.

....

Troy Dale Farris   **1/13/99**
Clark did not die in vain. I don't mean to offend you by saying that, but what I mean by that is, through his death, he led this man to God.

....

Kenneth Allen McDuff   **11/17/98**
I'm ready to be released. Release me.

....

Charlie Livingston   **11/21/97**
You all brought me here to be executed, not to make a speech. That's it.

....

Joe F. Gonzales, Jr.   **9/18/96**
There are people all over the world who face things worse than death on a daily basis, and in that sense I consider myself lucky.

....

Carl Johnson   **9/19/95**
I want the world to know that I'm innocent and that I've found peace. Let's ride.

....

Herman Clark, Jr.   **12/6/94**
I want to say that the bad evil man I was when I came to Death Row 13 years ago is no more — by the power of God.

....

Carl Kelly   **8/20/93**
I'm an African warrior, born to breathe, and born to die.

....

Leonel Torres Herrera   **5/12/93**
I am innocent, innocent, innocent. Make no mistake about this; something very wrong is taking place tonight.

....

G.W. Green   **11/12/91**
Let's do it, man. Lock and load. Ain't life a [expletive]?

....

Ignacio Cuevas   **5/21/91**
I'm going to a beautiful place. O.K., Warden, roll 'em. roll 'em.

....

Anthony Williams   **5/28/87**
Mother, I am sorry for all the pain I've caused you.

....

Kenneth A. Brock   **6/19/86**
I have no last words. I am ready.

MAD DOG, INC.

From the late sixties through the seventies and on into the eighties, a kindred group of writers, journalists, artists, politicos, troubadours, and raconteurs known as the Mad Dogs ran through Austin with rabid abandon. Gary "Jap" Cartwright and Edwin "Bud" Shrake, two former newspapermen in their literary ascendancies, were the ring leaders and charter members included writing luminaries Billy Lee Brammer, David Halberstam, Dan Jenkins, Larry L. King, and George Plimpton, along with the future Governor Ann Richards. Others would be initiated with a Mad Dog business card, a kiss on the cheek, some tequila, and two pesos. Willie Nelson and Jerry Jeff Walker, Mad Dogs both, were there to provide the soundtrack. Like the Outlaw Country music that wafted through the Austin ether, the Mad Dogs flowed merrily in and out of Austin's iconic haunts. There were the picnic tables at Scholz Garten, known as the Dearly Beloved Beer and Garden Party in Brammer's famous Austin-set novel, The Gay Place. There was the Raw Deal bar. And the Armadillo World Headquarters, where Cartwright and Shrake would arrive costumed as two flying Punzars, a pretend but performing troupe of Italian acrobats, accompanied by Richards, resplendently wigged and stuffed as Dolly Parton. Such gathering spots provided the Mad Dogs a hopped-up version of the Algonquin round table, and were where the divide between Austin's culturati and counterculturati was bridged. When not engaging in days-long competitive benders such as the historic one pitted against a visiting Hunter S. Thompson, or generally jacking with the establishment and raising hell like tomorrow wouldn't come, they wrote stunning and important pieces, sang beautiful and important songs, and served the public with aplomb. Maybe it was the other way around. A settling down was inevitable as the sunrise, but the mark had been made. For the last decade and half of Richards's life she and Shrake were inseparable, and when he died in 2009 they were reunited beneath a live oak tree on a hill in Texas State Cemetery in East Austin. They were joined by their friend Larry L. King in 2013. Mad Dogs, side by side again. Eternally.

TEXAS BLUES

Word-of-mouth nightclubs in East Austin were legendary stops along the southern Chitlin' Circuit. In the 1970's, these jukes inspired new venues that hosted post-segregation Blues revivalists, including Jimmie and Stevie Ray Vaughan. Few of the old clubs remain.

- ⤳ Victory Grill
- ⤳ Out Cross the Creek
- ⤳ Alexander's
- ⤳ Ernie's Chicken
- ⤳ Shack
- ⤳ The Derby
- ⤳ Charlie's Playhouse
- ⤳ Good Daddy's
- ⤳ The Rome Inn
- ⤳ The Black Queen

- ⤳ Sam's Showcase
- ⤳ Antone's
- ⤳ IL Club
- ⤳ One Knite
- ⤳ The Raw Deal
- ⤳ Flight 505
- ⤳ The Bottom Line
- ⤳ After Hours
- ⤳ La Cucaracha
- ⤳ TC's Lounge

- ⤳ The Gig
- ⤳ The Lamplight
- ⤳ Buffalo Gap
- ⤳ Soap Creek Saloon
- ⤳ Vulcan Gas Company
- ⤳ The Sit'n'Bull
- ⤳ The South Door
- ⤳ The Back Room

THEODORE ROOSEVELT

WASHINGTON
Oyster Bay, N.Y., Aug. 24th, 1901.

J.G. Booth, Esq.,

     Austin, Texas.

My dear Comrade Booth:

     I am in receipt of your letter of the 16th inst on behalf of Dr. James Byars. As you know, the Vice President has nothing to do with appointments unless he is asked by the President. But if the chance comes for me to say a good word for a member of the Texas Rangers, I shall most certainly do so.

Sincerely yours,

     Theodore Roosevelt

WHITE BASS

Every March, spawning white bass all over Central Texas
fight their way to cold moving river water. These rodeos
of foot-long silvery fish make for the best fly-fishing of the
calendar year. Jesse Griffiths, the Austin hunting guru
behind the Dai Due Supper Club and acclaimed author of
Afield: A Chef's Guide to Preparing and Cooking Wild
Game and Fish, *tells what to do when the redbud*
bloom signals the fish are on the run.

HOW TO CATCH AND COOK SPAWNING WHITE BASS

1. Wait until nightly lows are in the 60's, March or April.

2. Choose a day on a warming trend, not directly after a cold front, preferably on a weekday when most people are at work. After a good rain is usually good.

3. Get up early and prepare to walk in past the crowds.

4. Locate spot on a creek or where river attaches to a lake. White bass will bottle-neck the run, like a logjam or low water crossing. They rest here on their way upstream.

5. Fish this spot intensely, covering the entire area and all depths. White bass run in schools.

6. Fish with small lures in white, silver or chartreuse, and use a slow retrieve.

7. Keep your catch in the water, or put them directly on ice. White bass taste better if kept cool.

8. Fillet them as soon as possible, and save the delicious roe from the females.

9. Cook them with garlic or tomatoes and lots of fresh herbs. Artichokes are usually in season at the same time. Use them together.

10. Eat all you can and go back. The run is usually short. Take advantage.

"COMPLIMENTARY BALL"

Austin City Gazette
September 22, 1841

Friday evening last afforded another of those scenes of gay conviviality for which the city of Austin is so justly celebrated. Our citizens, highly gratified at the arrival of the Honorable Representatives from the infant Republic of Yucatan, and ever anxious to confer honor upon those whom it is due, by unanimous acclamation, contributed to give a splendid ball to Col. Martin Francisco Peraza, Commissioner Extraordinary, and Don Donacio G. Rejon, Secretary of Legation; and although but a short time was allowed for its preparation, everything was in keeping with that spirit of courteous liberality and national pride, which prompted them to offer such a practical demonstration of the feelings with which these messengers of liberty and independence were received in "the land of the free and the home of the brave."

The whole Capitol was brilliantly lighted up, and Senate Chamber tastefully decorated. Rich festoons of evergreens encircled the spacious walls; the one-starred banner of Texas was casting its brightness from the centre of the lofty ceiling; and above "the Chair," which served as an orchestra on this occasion, was seen, in beautiful transparency, a representation of the floating ensign of the Yucatan; while from the wreathed columns in its front, rose the solitary star, and the star-crowned cap of liberty, the appropriate national devices of the sister Republics of the South, connected by the very significant Spanish word "UNIDOS" written in large and beautiful letters of everygreen. The air was fresh and buoyant, the music was excellent, and the large and fashionable assemblage entered into the hilarities of the evening.

FILMED IN AUSTIN

Waiting for Guffman

Lonesome Dove

Capote

What's Eating Gilbert Grape

Boys Don't Cry

Slacker

The Life of David Gale

Hope Floats

Miss Congeniality

Kill Bill, Vol. 1

The Best Little Whorehouse
in Texas

Office Space

Grindhouse

Tree of Life

Once Upon a Time in Mexico

A Perfect World

Piranha

The Rookie

Secondhand Lions

Texas Chainsaw Massacre

Sin City

Spy Kids

True Grit

Varsity Blues

Stop-Loss

25th Hour

Courage Under Fire

Machete

ESPIONAGE

*Coded telegram
sent to Mexico from
Germans during WWI*

"We intend to begin on the first of February unrestricted submarine warfare. We shall endeavor in spite of this to keep the United States of America neutral. In the event of this not succeeding, we make Mexico a proposal of alliance on the following basis: make war together, make peace together, generous financial support and an understanding on our part that Mexico is to reconquer the lost territory in Texas, New Mexico, and Arizona. The settlement in detail is left to you. You will inform the President of the above most secretly as soon as the outbreak of war with the United States of America is certain and add the suggestion that he should, on his own initiative, invite Japan to immediate adherence and at the same time mediate between Japan and ourselves. Please call the President's attention to the fact that the ruthless employment of our submarines now offers the prospect of compelling England in a few months to make peace."

MOUNT BONNELL

The winter of 1839, General Sam Houston climbed the cedar-covered Mount Bonnell with a retired Texas Ranger, Mr. R.M. Williamson. It's recorded that as the two men looked out onto the gentle river and the varied woods and the pure air, Houston slapped Williamson on the back and said, "This must be the very spot where Satan took our Saviour to show and tempt him with the riches and beauties of the world." Once called Antoinette's Leap, after a young woman who was chased off the edge by natives who'd killed her fiancé, the limestone crag today gives hideout to underage beer-drinking and lonesome stargazing. Most consider it the finest view in many counties. Including Sam Houston's friend. "If Jesus Christ had been fallible," Williamson said to the General, "He would have accepted his Satanic majesty's proposition."

....

**A LETTER WRITTEN BY FIRST LADY
OF TEXAS, LUCADIA NILES PEASE,
ON FEB 27TH 1854**

Dear kind friends,

The country is beginning to look quite pretty now — a few days since we went with a small party to Mount Bonnell the great resort here — the road there is very pleasant, and the view from the mountain magnificent, at our feet the Colorado, breaking its way through the high rocky banks, its waters clear and beautiful, and the woods covered with cedar brightly green — and on the mountain is a shrub which they call mountain laurel, an evergreen with a purple flower...

Your aff. sister,
Lu

HARRY RANSOM CENTER

On the western edge of UT's campus, a seven-story public research center houses enough yellowing drafts and coffee-stained scribbles for ten thousand Saturdays. Walt Whitman. Carson McCullers. David Foster Wallace. Lord Byron. The list of authors, texts, and other literary stuff is obscene — in the best way.

- Edgar Allan Poe's writing desk
- Ezra Pound's copy of "The Waste Land," inscribed by T.S. Eliot
- Jack Kerouac's *On the Road* spiral writing journal
- William Shakespeare's 1623 *First Folio* [3 copies]
- James Joyce's personal, marked-up proofs for *Ulysses*
- 1,000 boxes of Norman Mailer's letters and manuscripts
- Official declaration from Napoleon Bonaparte
- Rare first edition of *Alice's Adventures in Wonderland*
- The Woodward and Bernstein Watergate papers
- Tennessee Williams' working manuscripts for *The Glass Menagerie* and *A Streetcar Named Desire*
- Two paintings by Frida Kahlo
- Dresses from *Gone With the Wind* film
- Props made by Salvador Dali

BARBECUE

Franklin's .... Feted as low-slow wunderkind — and kinda true
Micklethwait .... Upstart trailer and picnic tables a half-mile from Franklin
Mann's .... Smoky and fatty dancing together, free ice cream
John Mueller .... Famous BBQ grandson, trailer on East 6th
The Salt Lick .... Dripping Springs 'cue with mustard-vinegar sauce*
Louie Mueller .... Always-moist brisket, delicious pork in Taylor*
Smitty's .... Glazed ribs great, smoked sausage epic*
Black's .... Thick beef ribs, murmuring of awesome brisket*
Kreuz .... 550-seat Lockhart cathedral, pronounced "Krites"*
Snow's .... Cheery pit lady Tootsie sells out on Saturdays*
Short road trip but worth every mile

DROUGHT

The year 2011 was the driest year ever in state of Texas, which since October 2010 has been experiencing the worst drought on record. It's believed by climatologists that the shortage's height was October 2011, when eighty-eight percent of Texas was in "exceptional" drought, with wildfires, vanishing reservoirs and eight billion dollars in ruined crops. Some cattle ranchers even resorted to burning the spines off cactus to feed their herds, a tactic known as chamuscando. At a more micro level, the dire conditions appear through crumbling roads, grocery fluctuations and dying trees.

HOW TO CARE FOR TREES IN A DROUGHT

(1) Mark a drip line around rim of outer branches

(2) Trickle water once a week in three-foot area straddling drip line

(3) Let ground dry between your waterings

(4) Water the same area every week, getting water to outer roots for best care

(5) Do not water the base of the trunk of mature trees

(6) Do not dig holes to water more deeply, as it dries out roots.

(7) Spread mulch three inches deep, keeping four inches from trunk

(8) Watch for symptoms like wilt, leaf blistering, powdery mildew, yellowing, cankers and burls

(9) Consult with ISA certified arborists on soil nutrition and fertilization

---

"A ROW DIE"
Texas Sentinel
February 11, 1841

We noticed, a few days since, a fellow dashing about with a huge Bowie knife protruding from his bosom. We advise him to exchange this weapon for a corn cob; he will find the latter much lighter and more convenient to wear, than the Bowie knife, and just as useful in respectable society.

MAPS

Hand-illustrated maps to tell secrets about swimming holes, dive bars, the movies, live music, trailer tacos and the city's biggest ideas

SWIMMIN'
HOLES

KRAUSE
SPRINGS

HAMILTON POOL

WIMBERLY
THE BLUE
HOLE

COMAL
RIVER

NEW
BRAUNFELS

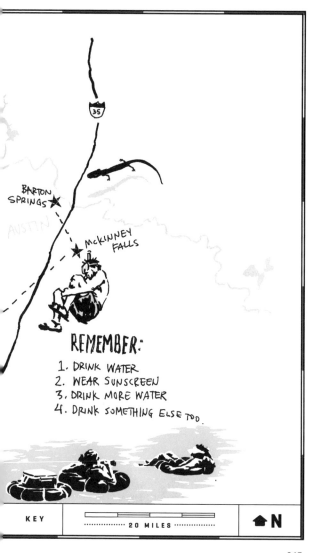

35

BARTON
SPRINGS

AUSTIN

McKINNEY
FALLS

REMEMBER:

1. DRINK WATER
2. WEAR SUNSCREEN
3. DRINK MORE WATER
4. DRINK SOMETHING ELSE TOO.

KEY   20 MILES   ⬆N

MAPS

⫸ SWIMMING HOLES ⫷

When the city begins to boil, locals rush to find sweet relief in dozens of slow-moving rivers and spring-fed pools — all fed by an artesian aquifer.

HAMILTON POOL

Inside Balcones Canyonlands, the otherworldly-aqua pool sits inside a 50-foot wall grotto [the limestone caved in a long time ago] and, when it rains, there's waterfall runoff from the creek above. Open year-round, $8. *Hamilton Pool Road [FM 3238]*

KRAUSE SPRINGS

Owned by a Spicewood family for 50-plus years, this lush weekender's spot gets pretty crowded during the summer, but the pool's beautiful enough that you don't notice. Open year-round, $6. *404 Krause Spring Rd*

BARTON SPRINGS

The revered urban sanctuary gets 30 million gallons of 68-degree water a day from Parthenia, the underground font on the south edge of Zilker Park. Open year-round, $3 entry. *2101 Barton Springs Rd*

MCKINNEY FALLS

Minutes from downtown, the state park has gnarly limestone formations where Onion Creek — when the state's not experiencing serious drought — flows over two sets of falls. Open year-round, $6. *5808 McKinney Falls Pkwy*

THE BLUE HOLE

Lazy cypresses lean out over this movie-perfect, spring-fed oasis, not far from downtown Wimberley. Extra points for gainers off the rope swing. Open Memorial Day-Labor Day. *333 Blue Hole Ln*

COMAL RIVER

The 2.5-mile tuber's tributary in New Braunfels is clear and green and home to the Schlitterbahn, a German-inspired water park on 16 riverside acres. *texastubes.com*

LOCAL EXPERTS *John Hart Asher works as an environmental designer at the Lady Bird Johnson Wildflower Center, a native plants research champion founded in 1982.*

⋙ DIVE BARS ⋘

No city in America does the dinghy hole-in-the-wall quite like ATX, where beer from a tap might be considered fancy and Jerry Jeff rules the jukebox.

LONGBRANCH INN

Patrons of this patina-rich saloon-style staple near the Victory Grill raise their whiskey shots nightly to the stuffed beaver behind the bar. *1133 E 11th*

DEEP EDDY CABARET

What used to be a bait shop and grocery near the namesake spring-fed pool is now a beloved watering hole, full of knick-knacks and friendly barkeeps. *2315 Lake Austin Blvd*

GINNY'S LITTLE LONGHORN

Nothing quite like Chicken Shit Bingo on Sundays with Sissy the rooster doing his thing as the tiny beershack hoops and hollers like it's the Super Bowl. *5434 Burnet Rd*

THE WHITE HORSE

Young buck on the scene, this nightspot is already a favorite among local bands, partly because the co-owner is as good a banjo player as he is a bartender.

HORSESHOE LOUNGE

Once an American Legion outpost off South Lamar, the U-shaped bar, circa 1965, is a neighborhood anchor. And the shuffleboard is the best in town. *2034 S Lamar*

LIBERTY BAR

Great beer selection inside and a dog-friendly backyard with picnic tables out back, made much better with pork buns from chef Paul Qui's East Side King trailer. *1618 1/2 E 6th St*

SCOOT INN

This railroader's hang may look like a caved-in barn, but it's been booking live music since 1871 — and sporting serious skeeball playing for decades. *1308 E 4th St*

LOCAL EXPERT *The upstart Austin Beerworks is all about canned beer, what they call super-fresh mini-kegs. Plus, for tubers, they float. Try the crisp Pearlsnap Pils. austinbeerworks.com*

DEEP EDDY CABARET

GINNY'S LITTLE LONGHORN

GINNY'S LITTLE LONGHORN

DEEP EDDY ★

BARS

HORSE SHOE LOUNGE

★

LOUNGE

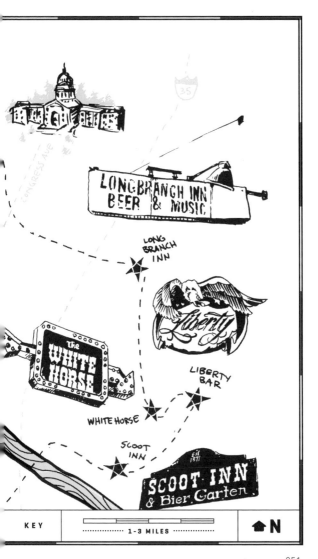

LONG BRANCH INN
BEER & MUSIC

LONG
BRANCH
INN

Liberty

The WHITE HORSE

LIBERTY
BAR

WHITE HORSE

SCOOT
INN

Est
1871
SCOOT INN
& Bier Garten

KEY   1-3 MILES   ⬆N

DAZED & CONFUSED
★

Film

LONESOME DOVE
★

TEXAS CHAINSAW MASSACRE

FRIDAY NIGHT LIGHTS

SLACKER

AUSTIN

TREE OF LIFE

KEY

A WAYS

N

≫ FILM ≪

From Linklater devotees to SXSW's festival cred,
Austin's become a laidback alternative to Hollywood's glitzy ways.

THE TEXAS CHAIN SAW MASSACRE (1974)

The classic slasher by Tobe Hooper was bootstrapped in Round Rock using local actors and blood from a nearby slaughterhouse. It grossed $30 million. *Locations: Small 1900's farm house on Quick Hill Road*

LONESOME DOVE (1989)

In the canon of Texas, McMurtry's novel is *Don Quixote*. And the miniseries wasn't all hat and no cattle either. Lockhart shop, Texas Hatters sure did their part with Robert Duvall's headpiece. *Locations: Hill Country, South Tx*

SLACKER (1991)

Richard Linklater's ode to Austin's funky zeitgeist premiered at the Dobie Theater in 1991 and would flick hundreds of cultural dominos. *Locations: Sound Exchange, Half-Priced Books, Mount Bonnell, Continental Club and more*

DAZED AND CONFUSED (1993)

This was Linklater's *Fast Times at Ridgemont High*: A Zeppelin-infused coming-of-age at the moontower that gave McConaughey his scene-stealing Hollywood intro. *Locations: Top Notch Restaurant, West Enfield Park, Americana library branch*

FRIDAY NIGHT LIGHTS (2006–2011)

Critics cheered Coach T, but it was Texas-forever tragic hero Tim Riggins that made this show something like Shakespeare playing in the spread. *Locations: Broken Spoke, Ray's Bar-B-Q, The Landing Strip*

THE TREE OF LIFE (2011)

Austinite Terrance Malick's gorgeous head-scratcher is set partly in nearby Smithville, a town just stuck-in-time-enough for the auteur's vision. Plus it had great trees. *Locations: Barton Springs, The Capitol, The bats*

LOCAL EXPERT *Paul Berg and Kristin Johansen-Berg dreamed up Arts + Labor in a garage apartment in 2004. Today, the award-winning agency does film work for Dell, UT and Shiner Bock. arts-and-labor.com*

*With massively popular music festivals and a wild heritage of genre-bending
clubs, Austin's reputation for tunes every-night-of-the-year is still rocking.*

THE MOHAWK

Owned by the folks that run Fun
Fun Fun, this seven-year-old Red
River club has a committed
following ["All are welcome"]
and by-far the best green room
in the city. 921 *Red River St,
mohawkaustin.com*

AUSTIN CITY LIMITS

In 1976, the television series first
rolled tape on UT's campus, fake
city skyline and all, and almost
40 years later, Terry Lickona's
brainchild is a bonafide American
icon. *acltv.com*

CACTUS CAFÉ

The UT student union has
won a decade's worth of Austin
Music Awards — its acoustics
are legendary — so locals freaked
when officials talked of shutting
it down. 2247 *Guadalupe St,
cactuscafe.org*

BEERLAND

We dig rock clubs with graffiti-
scarred bathrooms, Shiner-splat-
tered floors and stages the size of
truck beds. Karaoke Mondays, too.
711 *Red River St, beerlandtexas.com*

SAXON PUB

Chosen hometown haunt of Bob
Schneider, W.C. Clark and dozens
others, who appreciate the inti-
mate atmosphere and that South
Austin Music is next-door. 1320
South Lamar, thesaxonpub.com

CONTINENTAL CLUB

The always-dark classic has been a
private 1950s supper club, redneck
beer joint, punk incubator, and
Texas blues shrine — and it's
never stopped revering Elvis. 1315
S Congress, continentalclub.com

OLD SETTLERS FESTIVAL

Americana and folk music
shindig at the Salt Lick Pavilion,
30 bands and four stages, plus
jamming and skills sessions with
master players. April,
oldsettlersmusicfest.com

LOCAL EXPERTS *Rosa Madriz works with Transmission Events to
organize Fun Fun Fun Fest, a three-day anti-festival started in 2006
to be more about indie and underground than big-name headliners.*

MUSIC

THINGS YOU NEED
TO BE A MUSIC
VENUE IN AUSTIN:

1. ELECTRICITY *

AUSTIN
CITY
LIMITS

CESAR CHAVEZ

LAMAR

SAXON PUB

OLD SETTLERS
FESTIVAL

THE
Continental
CLUB

THE CONTINENTAL CLUB

CACTUS CAFE

35

Mohawk

BEER LAND TEXAS

THE MOHAWK

BEERLAND

NOT ACTUALLY REQUIRED

KEY

·········· 1.5 MILES ··········

N

TACODELI

35

ROSITA'S

EL POLLO
RICO

LA MICHOACANA
MEAT MARKET

VERACRUZ
AL NATURAL

TACOS

TAQUERIA
LOS
JALISCIENSES

1. a piece of metal.

things you need
to cook tacos

pro tip:
use the tortilla
as an oven mitt

2. heat.

KEY   1 MILE   N

⇒ TACOS ⇐

Barbecue rivalries get the press, but the burgeoning taco scene in town is heating up, from opposite-of-fancy trailers to a stepped-up fast casual mini-chain.

VERACRUZ ALL NATURAL
Small trailer fenced in with thatch hut tables, well-known for homemade tortillas and guacamole, delicious juices and fresh salsa bowl. Rachael Ray loves this tiny spot. *1704 E Cesar Chavez*

LA MICHOACANA MEAT MARKET
Serve yourself the autentico barbacoa at the taco bar inside the bustling market, or stop by the butcher counter to make your own adventure over an open flame [see map]. *1917 E 7th St*

TAQUERIA LOS JALISCIENCES
Early-risers grab sacks of these eastside tacos at the red-roofed corner restaurant en route to construction sites and never forget to load up on the salsa verde. *6903 Airport Blvd*

EL POLLO RICO
Walk-up spot is super-cheap and grills legendary whole chickens, sautées sweet onions that'll make you weep, and finishes off everything with a perfect squeezed lime. Do not drive past this place - even if you've already eaten. *1945 E Oltorf St*

ROSITA'S
Hard to find a better version of the taco al pastor in Austin. They make their thick flour tortillas in-house, fill them with generous heapings of tender meat, sprinkle with cilantro and sell them four-for-five-bucks. Big lunch. *1911 E Riverside Dr*

TACODELI
Some might call this a "gringo taco" stop — but who really cares — their menu is chockfull of legitimacy, from the Fundido sirloin to grilled Gulf shrimp to veggie Space Cowboy. These are modern Austin tacos done best. *Three spots, including 1500 Spyglass*

LOCAL EXPERTS *Jack Sanders' Design Build Adventure crew rock one-of-a-kind architectural projects, from treehouses to airstream redo's. designbuildadventure.com*

⚛ BIG IDEAS ⚛

*From how the world eats to the latest tech start-ups to gridiron
X's and O's, Austin's always been game to challenge the status quo.*

WHOLE FOODS
College dropout John Mackey's vision for sustainable and organic — adjectives rarely used in 1978 — has grown from an apartment idea into 340 stores and $11 billion in annual sales.

DELL
It's the modern American Dream: UT freshman builds homemade computers, wins government contracts, becomes a billionaire, gets name on baseball stadium.

COSMIC COWBOYS
The folk-country-hippie hodge-podge that was 1970s Austin steeped a funkiness that flat-out demanded a Grateful-Dead-and-Wranglers kind of name, and this was it. Thank you, Michael Martin Murphey.

BARB WIRE
Ten years before some guy in Illinois patented it, Swiss immigrant John Grinninger, who lived on Waller Creek, twisted wires with bits of iron and glass — the first appearance of "Devil's rope" in America.

LIVESTRONG
With over $500 million raised since 1997, the scandal-ridden racer's eponymous charity has pushed serious cancer research and sold 80 million yellow wristbands in its support of survivors.

SXSW
When a trio at the *Austin Chronicle* hatched the original shindig in 1987, few imagined a ten-day mecca for music, film and "interactive" — what's become the modern launching pad for tech darlings.

WISHBONE OFFENSE
In 1968, UT ran the first "pulley bone" triple-option, sparking a 30-game win streak, leading to two titles and causing Bear Bryant to play copycat in Tuscaloosa.

LOCAL EXPERTS *In entrepreneur-crazy Austin, the Capitol Factory takes select tech start-ups on a 10-week crash course in customer traction, led by an impressive list of angel investors and business mentors.*

BIG

ideas

D.I.Y. =

1. DO IT YOURSELF
2. DRAWN IT YESTERDAY
3. DALLAS IS YUCKY

WHOLE FOODS
MARKET

WHOLE FOOD:
- - - ★

COSMIC COWBOYS

DON'T FORGET
THE TACO CANNON

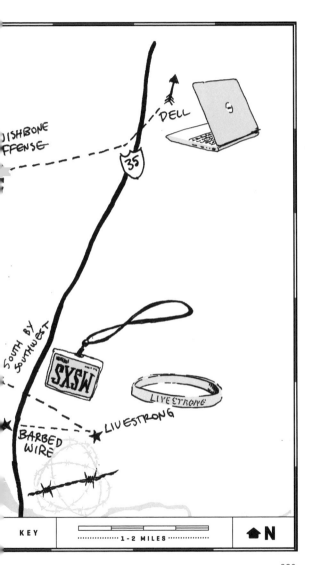

WISHBONE
OFFENSE

DELL

35

SOUTH BY
SOUTHWEST

SXSW

LIVESTRONG

LIVESTRONG

BARBED
WIRE

KEY   1-2 MILES   ◆N

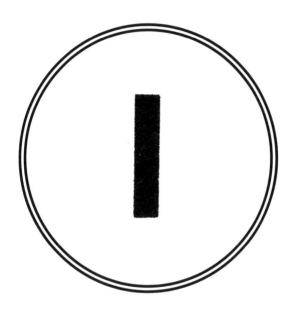

INTERVIEWS

Fifteen conversations with locals about making boots, rebuilding an old motel, growing up with a pitmaster, exploring the Texas myth and more

»» TODD SANDERS ««

NEON ARTIST

A signmaker on his first trip to Austin, falling in love and why he sees neon everywhere

THIS IS MY NEON BONEYARD. I bought it in 1997.

....

THE BIG CHICKEN is from Waco. They wanted $2,000 dollars and crane truck fees to move it over. I paid them $100 a month for 20 months.

....

I WAS LIVING in a trailer park behind Maria' s Tacos.

....

THERE WAS NO NEON on South First then. It was just dark. All of the houses had two junk cars in the yard and grass growing up four feet tall.

....

THE FIRST CARTOONS anyone saw were animated neon signage. Where the hobo is walking or the girl's dancing or the dog's wagging his tail. They even put neon on the Eiffel Tower at one point.

....

ON A ROAD TRIP I pulled into Austin and saw all these cool neon signs spinning. I felt like I was in the land of the misfit toys.

....

I TURNED TO MY BUDDY and I said, "Man, I'm living here the rest of my life."

....

I MET MY WIFE because she walked in to buy a sign from me.

....

THE THINGS I LOVE aren't dated. They're timeless.

....

THE AURORA BOREALIS, that's neon lighting up the sky. They freeze atmosphere, scrape off the crude and take the neon.

....

NEON'S A PART OF US. It speaks to me like a full moon.

....

ONE NIGHT the place was completely dark. We walked in and I picked up an extension chord. I plugged in a sign that said *Sarah will you marry me*. And she said yes.

⫸ EVAN SMITH ⫷

EDITOR-IN-CHIEF

A newsman's thoughts on the Texas myth, Presidential politics and rethinking journalism

I'VE ALWAYS BEEN an editor. I think there's a personality aspect to it. I'm enough of an asshole to think I know better.

OFTEN A WRITER gets so deep into a subject they can no longer remember what it was like not to be an expert.

EVERY PIECE I ever edited in 18 years at *Texas Monthly* was the same piece. Every piece that runs is a piece about the Texas myth.

INDEPENDENT, a free spirit, liberated from the shackles of whatever attempts to confine you. It's a frontier mentality. It's an unwillingness to take shit from other people.

THE STEREOTYPE has been overplayed by media. That everybody in Texas is a shitkicker who rides horseback through downtown, and they have buttons in their house to execute people.

The reality of Texas is both complicated and simple.

PERRY NEVER ACTUALLY said, "I support secession." He gave legitimacy to a conversation, yes. And after that, the Hutchison people said we have this thing won. And the Perry people said we have this thing won.

HE HAS BEEN exceedingly good at seeing around corners in his career.

GUY FALLS OUT of a sixth story window and lands on his feet. It's like the whole Presidential race was that season of *Dallas* when Victoria realized the whole thing was a dream. Like nothing ever happened.

I HAVE extraordinary memories of 2000. Thirty-six days. One night I walked into the Governor's mansion, and there was Dick Cheney, unshaven. There was Condelezza Rice. All these national press guys, picking at a buffet line. Then, Bush walks in. He had on a baseball cap and a field coat, jeans and boots. He had a boil on his face that we all joked was in the shape of Florida. He saw me and he pointed and he said, "Big boy!" It was a very weird time.

....

HE'D NEVER GET elected again. Bush was too moderate.

....

TEXAS IS a blood red state in a country that is center-right. The Democratic party here is effectively the third party in a two-party state.

....

I JOKE that I used to be a journalist. When I got here in 1991, there were still two daily papers in Dallas and Houston and San Antonio and El Paso. What I do at the *Tribune* is pay

for journalism.

....

BUILD A TIME MACHINE and go back to *Esquire* in the 60s if you want to just be a writer. What I want is a Swiss Army knife of journalism skills.

....

I TOLD MY WIFE not long after quit *Texas Monthly* to start the *Tribune*, "If this doesn't work out I'm employable."

....

IT WAS DECEMBER of 1991. I'd written to the editor of *Texas Monthly* and said, "I'll sweep up, clean the kitchen. Just get me a job."

....

I HAVE extraordinarily specific memories of that time.

....

TELLING A STORY. There's a million wrong ways to do it. You just have to find one right way.

Evan Smith co-founded The Texas Tribune *with veteran political journalist, Ross Ramsey, and Austin venture capitalist, John Thornton, in 2009. Cobbling together a mix of respected newspaper-folk and rising stars, the nonpartisan, nonprofit* Tribune *won two Edward. R. Murrow Awards in its first year online. In 2011, the media start-up registered 4.0 million page views and struck up a content partnership with* The New York Times.

»› LIZ LAMBERT ‹«

HOTEL MAKER

The style impresario on being different, growing up in far West Texas and the last days of the San Jose

I USED TO JUST SIT on a bar stool at the Continental and stare out across Congress at the San Jose. And before I knew it, I had it. My mom co-signed the note just before the owners listed it in the Chinese newspaper.

DUCT TAPE AND GUM held the hotel together.

ROOMS WERE THIRTY BUCKS a night. Nobody who stayed there had cars or luggage or came out during the day. I was pulling crack pipes out of the vacuum cleaner.

I ABSOLUTELY didn't know what I was doing. I figured I could redo it room by room. It was faulty thinking.

WE REOPENED during SXSW fully booked. There was no soft opening. Actually there was a problem with the plumbing and the sewage backed up in all the rooms and flooded an inch.

IT'S CONSTANT. A hotel is open 365 days a year.

I'M A CHILD of the Cosmic Cowboy. It's the place where the West Texas in me gets to meet the hippie.

I GREW UP IN ODESSA, and my granddad was a rancher. Ranchers didn't drive trucks much back then. He drove a Buick. It was covered in dust.

HE DIDN'T HAVE an office in town, so he'd always go to the local hotel and take meetings. He'd sit on the couches and read the newspaper, smoke a cigar and get his hair cut.

I HAVE A STRONG memory of those days.

GABRIEL PERALES

BASEBALL COMMISSIONER

A local realtor on Fernando Valenzuela, his love of America's pastime and La Liga de Hispana

ONCE YOU'RE OUT of high school, baseball is hard to find.

THERE IS A MAN named Pancho. He is the owner-manager of a team called the Dodgers, famous all through Mexico. They'd fizzled, so he called me to see if I wanted to play a friendly. I called a few people, and fifty players showed up.

BASEBALL IS baseball. What was missing when La Liga de Hispana started was organization. You'd have an umpire in jeans and a hat, sipping on a beer. We stopped all that.

THE FIRST YEAR a team called the Riales had a 49-year-old pitcher, a lefty, ...who'd played several professional seasons in Mexico. Boy, he did magic. Went undefeated all the way through the playoffs.

WE DIDN'T EVEN HAVE a real backstop then. It was chicken wire and the infield was all sand.

THE DAY OF OUR first championship game, my friend said he'd never seen so many Mexicans in one place — other than at a dance.

THE COPS showed up, but to my surprise, they offered to help direct traffic.

BEFORE GAMES, we raise both flags and play both national anthems.

I WAS RAISED in El Paso, and my favorite player was the great Fernando Valenzuela. Every week we visited my Grandpa in Mexico. Talks with him went like this: How was I doing, how was he doing, and how was Fernando Valenzuela doing.

⫸ MICHAEL MULLER ⫷

MUSICIAN

🔖 The Balmorhea cofounder's ideas about Texas settlers, songwriting and new beginnings

BALMORHEA. *Bal-mor-ray.* It's a small town in West Texas. Mostly desert. In hindsight, it might not have been the best idea. No one ever pronounces it right.

WE PRINTED 1,000 copies of the first Balmorhea record. It took a long time to get rid of those.

THE SONGS WERE SIMPLE, very stark. Some piano and guitar, a few field recordings here and there. Words never seemed to fit.

OUR VERY FIRST SHOW was at Beerland in Austin.

ALL IS SILENT, ALL IS WILD is about Texas settlers. We found an old 1880s journal, and it set a rustic and dark tone.

HE WAS COMING from Tennessee, and in one part, he's looking over a bluff and writing about the beauty of the land and the openness. But he's also frightened and intimidated by how wild it seems. That juxtaposition felt right.

BEFORE WE WRITE, the very first thing we do is to establish a feeling.

WE'VE USED THE SOUND of moving trains. We've recorded cicadas in Rob's yard. And in the fall, the leaves fall and make tiny little clapping sounds. We recorded that too.

A BRIDGE BETWEEN two of our songs is just a recording of a café in Vienna. You can hear an opera practicing next-door.

FANS IN EUROPE always ask us if we know George Bush and Chuck Norris.

THEY HEAR where we're from and they're always curious.

»» THOMAS HENDERSON ««

PRO ATHLETE

The retired Dallas Cowboy on segregation, summers on an oil rig and being called "Hollywood"

I NEVER HEARD IT. I never saw it. Never saw my parents embarrassed, never heard my daddy called Boy. I didn't even know there was segregation.

THERE WERE NO fires, no fights, no police dogs. Martin Luther King was radical to us.

THE DAY WHITMAN started shooting at UT, I was on campus, playing hooky from school. I ran towards East Austin and saw police cars and, for a moment, I was worried they were after me.

SUMMER OF 1972, I went to work on a rig in the Gulf. Twelve hours a day, carrying 100-pound bags of concrete. The transformation was incredible. I went from the lanky skinny boy to Incredible Hulk.

I NEVER KNEW my real father until I became a Dallas Cowboy.

TOM LANDRY and the Cowboys were looking for diamonds in the rough. And I had no fear. They really liked that.

I WENT TO THREE SUPER BOWLS in my first four years. I started dating a Pointer Sister and hanging out with Richard Pryor. That's when the nickname came up.

MY ONLY REGRET in life is drugs. Embarrassing my mother is the most disgrace I've ever felt.

BUT THE GREATEST single thing that ever happened to Thomas Henderson was getting sober. Not the Texas lottery.

WHEN IT STARTED, I bought $100 in tickets and won $28 million. Texas lottery.

I COULD HAVE gotten the whole amount spread over 25 years, but who wants to go to the mailbox everyday.

MELBA WHATLEY

CONSERVATIONIST

A Waller Creek champion on staying young, going big and her dreams about Yo-Yo Ma

AUSTIN IS not a city of urban beauty. It is a city of natural beauty. You can find it anywhere.

BEAUTY IS something for all people.

EVERY SUNDAY I take my dog Hector up Mount Bonnell. We walk up all those steps and stand at the top.

PEOPLE IN AUSTIN AREN'T AFRAID to be old but it's a place where you can stay young for a really long time. There are so many young ideas here. It's inspiring.

I WISH I COULD remember who told me, but they said, "Austin isn't critical. And that's why it can do what it wants."

THE WALLER CREEK project reconnects Austin from UT to Lady Bird Lake. It's a connecting tissue. It binds the city together. This isn't Millennium Park. It can't be, and it shouldn't.

THE ONE FAUX PAS that exists in Austin is being overdressed.

THE PROJECT IS situated along a flood plain. So, in order to get around this, the city is building a tunnel. If only you could see this tunnel, it is huge.

IF YOU ASKED ME AGAIN if I wanted to lead an international design contest while also running a landmark conservancy movement at the same time, I would say, "Are you crazy?" We didn't know what we were doing when we got started.

THIS WILL BE A defining movement for Austin. No project of this scale has ever happened in the city.

WE ARE an urban place. If there's no respite, no place for family's to go to watch trees bloom, we've lost something important.

I HOPE Yo-Yo Ma wants to come.

STEVE WERTHEIMER

CLUB OWNER

The Blueshound on old Austin haunts, running the Continental Club and the Grey Ghost

I GOT TO AUSTIN in 1976 and I immediately fell in love.

....

THE FABULOUS Thunderbirds were playing at the Rome Inn every Monday. Stevie Vaughan doing Sunday nights or Tuesdays. He was just a kid. Doug Sahm, W.C. Clark, the Cobras. It was an incredible time. I'd be there four nights a week.

....

WHEN I GOT OUT OF UT, I was a CPA. I had an office up in an ivory tower in downtown Austin and every day I looked out and wondered what I was doing up there. I wanted to be at the Rome Inn.

....

WHEN I BOUGHT the Continental Club, it was rough. And there was nothing on South Congress.

....

WE SCRUBBED the place down. Stripped it down to the bare walls and found the murals.

THERE WERE A BUNCH of black and white photos left behind. Pictures of the 50's, when the club was coat-and-tie, hoity-toity, women in cocktail dresses.

....

I READ IN THE PAPER that there was a birthday party for this old piano player, the Grey Ghost. Roosevelt Williams. Everybody thought he was dead.

....

MR. WILLIAMS had been driving a bus for 20 years in Bastrop when I met him. He was 86. No one knew him, but he was one of the last great Texas barrelhouse piano players.

....

I'D GO to his house every week and try to talk him into getting out and playing.

....

IT WAS MAGIC.

....

GUYS LIKE HIM have become my family. I give them all the credit for making our club. All I am is the steward.

»» LEANN MUELLER ««

PHOTOGRAPHER

A pitmaster's daughter on shooting barbecue, her family and the last time she took her dad's picture

WHEN DAD CAME HOME, even after he showered, he had that hint of barbecue on him. And the man could not get his nails clean, ever.

....

MY GRANDFATHER Louis opened a grocery store and started barbecuing in the alley.

....

IT'S A HARD JOB, unforgiving, demanding. But it's always been the most important thing in my family.

....

WE didn't go on many vacations.

BARBECUE is something I just can't get away from, no matter how hard I try, even if I wanted to.

....

MY BROTHER WAYNE runs Louis Mueller now. John just opened a new place. And I own a barbecue trailer in Austin.

....

THE LAST TIME I saw my dad was when I photographed him for the magazine.

TEXAS MONTHLY had approached me to shoot the top five places in Texas. Smitty's, Kreuz, Snow's, Luling, and my dad's place. There was a lot of pressure.

....

UH, I MEAN, they're all good. You know - I like them, I do - but I know my favorite.

....

YOU COULD EAT a piece of my dad's lean and it was just as tender as the moist. You're always going to like what you grew up with.

....

I TRIED NOT TO TELL anyone until after the portraits were done that my dad was Bobby Mueller. They would have thought I was stealing their secrets.

....

ONCE WHEN I WAS living in Brooklyn, my dad calls and says, I'm coming to New York. He'd won a James Beard award, and he didn't even know what it was all about.

»» JULIE BLAKESLEE ««

GARDEN DESIGNER

A landscape lover on Hill Country style, herb strategy and the healing power of dirt

THE EARTH needs a lot from you.

WHEN I GOT TO AUSTIN, there were all of these people, all this money, working ninety-hour weeks and channeling intelligence and energy into the city.

BUT IF YOU LOOK LIKE you put too much money into anything here, people say, "Whoa, whoa, whoa! Dial it back."

A WOMAN BUILT a contemporary house on 37 acres and she told us she wanted it to be brown, like nothing happened. It's unnatural if there is any green. She found that beautiful.

I DON'T LIKE TO SEE too much color on the landscape. It freaks me out.

I GET MY HANDS DIRTY, every day. It's gross, and it's fabulous.

MY GRANDPA was a landscape designer and gardener. He taught us to grow. So when my dog died, I dove into my garden for two months straight.

I USE SMELL all of the time when I'm designing. All of the herbs, everything that has aromatic foliage. You want to plant where your body will brush it, so the plants go with you.

EDGES NEED TO BLEED in together and be a little scraggly.

THE HILL COUNTRY is absolutely beautiful. The way it sounds when the wind is ripping through the grasses. Gorgeous.

IN THE SPRING, bluebonnets explode, and then, in six weeks, they all go away, and you just have this memory.

PEOPLE HERE GET really attached to the outside. I think it's the light.

MICHAEL MCNAMARA

COLLEGE STUDENT

A Silver Spur shares the history and proper handling of a famous Longhorn steer

HE'S A 2,000 POUND steer with horns six feet wide, so the bottom line is that if Bevo wants to do something, he's going to do it.

THE HANDLERS will walk up to him with the halter, but he's pretty good at avoiding it. It can take a long time if he's in a bad mood.

HE PLAYS GOOD DEFENSE, unlike our football team this year.

THAT GAME WHEN Colt got hurt, that was really rough on us.

YOU SEE VIDEOS on YouTube of guys trying to run Colorado's buffalo, and they just get dragged across the field.

BACK IN THE 1950'S, it snowed the day of a game. Bevo had never seen snow before. So he freaked out and sprinted down the middle of the field, dragging two handlers behind him. People were coming down from the stands trying to corral him.

ANYTIME WE'RE DRIVING in the truck, you get people honking at you and throwing their horns up. We've had cops pull up next to us and take pictures.

THAT'S WHAT WE call him, Stud. He's known as Bevo, but that's what Mr. and Mrs. Baker call him. Stud.

EVERYONE WEARS Wranglers and a burnt orange button down, short sleeved. We get them tailored at Gassane's where President Bush got his suits tailored.

OUR COWBOY HATS come from Texas Hatters, the same place that made Stevie Ray Vaughan's.

YOU CAN spot a Spur on campus by his hat and his boots. I'll have those boots and that hat for as long as I live.

»» FRANCIS FISCHER ««

SWIMMER

One local's thought on why Barton Springs matters, swimming with ducks and talk of the cold water

THE WATER COMES OUT at supposedly 68 degrees. Which is just fine, keeps the numbers down to tolerable amounts. If you've come from Chicago as I did, or spent a lot of time in Cape Cod, that's rather refreshing.

I'M 86 YEARS OLD. I swim only one lap now, but it's a quarter of a mile. I swim on my back, watching the bird life and clouds.

SEVERAL YEARS AGO, I came by with a banana plant and a spade and the lifeguard said, "What are you going to do?" And I said, "I'm going to plant banana plants in the men's dressing area." He said, "Cool." That's Austin.

SOMETIMES MEN sunbathe in the nude, lying on the grass.

SEE KIDS SAYING "Hey Dad, look there's a pineapple growing on that bush!" They never knew where a pineapple came from other than the grocery store.

IT'S CRYSTAL CLEAR water. Vegetation grows in the bottom of the pool, and there are fish, turtles, bird life, herons.

WE SWIM three feet from the ducks and they just look back at you.

I'M NOT GOING to philosophize about "back to nature," but there is some of that.

YOU DON'T GET to know which ones are millionaires and which ones only go on free days. It's only "Good morning" and ""Did you see the bougainvillea?"

I'VE BEEN THERE longer than any lifeguards. They all nod their heads and defer, pleasantly.

I CANNOT SWIM in a chlorinated pool now. It just stinks to me.

JOSHUA BINGAMAN

BOOTMAKER

The Helm Boots founder on family heritage, the Godfather and making heirloom products

I HAD ONE GRANDFATHER who was an ambulance driver and one was an auto mechanic. I still have their Red Wings.

WHEN MY BROTHER and I opened a shoe store in San Francisco 13 years ago, he was the sneaker guy. I was into boots. We called it the Subterranean Shoe Room.

WHEN WE CAME to Austin, we opened a small cafe called Progress that we loved.

WHEN I HAD some free time, I visited my aunt in Istanbul and met a guy who did handmade shoes in a factory.

I DREW MY IDEAS like a 3rd grader. That's how Helm Boots started.

I WANTED SOMETHING that was part military boot, part dress shoe and part old-time football cleat.

FASTER AND BIGGER isn't always better. But I was focused on making a big brand. Then I realized that I didn't want that. I wanted one store, one community.

DESIGNED IN TEXAS, made in Maine.

I LOVE THE WORD 'LAST.' A last is a mold of the right and left boot in every size you are going to make.

IT'S LIKE GODFATHER stuff. You have to be trusted. It's not just writing a check. The guy in Maine said, We aren't going on a date. We're putting a ring on it.

YES. It's skin. It's a cow. But we're taking 20 things and bringing them all into one. These are boots you'll give to your kid one day.

MY WIFE'S against me keeping more than 30 pairs of boots in the closet.

⟫ SUZI SOSA ⟪

SOCIAL ENTREPRENEUR

A teacher-innovator on what makes a good idea, Whole Foods and the power of fear

JUST BEING NEW is not enough. Innovations are ideas that are disruptive.

FEAR IS A STRONG anchor. It gives people a reference point to make decisions. But you have to let go.

WHERE does innovation come from? It comes from the misfits.

PATAGONIA, Starbucks, Zappos, The Container Store, Whole Foods. They ask, "How can we help our suppliers make more money?" And they mean it.

IF SOMEONE ELSE is getting something, then I'm losing out. Conscious capitalism says that's bullshit.

ONCE YOU LET GO of your fear, you find a new way.

TECHNOLOGY is blasting everything open. The more people know, the more the empowered and activated they become.

A FRIEND OF MINE says we place little bets. We wait to see what wins. And those ideas get to critical mass.

DESIGN THINKING IS the scientific method, just packaged for the 21st century. Inspiration is observation, ideation is hypothesis, iteration is the experiment.

ONE STUDENT of mine thinks everyone should have access to naps. So she came up with this snooze cruiser idea where people rent berths, ride around town and take naps.

THE IRREVERENCE of Texas and the weirdness of Austin — both are essential.

IF IT'S SHINY and nobody's going to use it, then who cares?

MY FAVORITE IDEAS are always the crazy ones.

≫ PAUL QUI ≪

CHEF

The East Side King on his origins in Austin, his first food trailer and the magic of McDonald's fries

MY PLAN IN 2003 was to go to culinary school in Austin, then get a job in a badass New York kitchen. Tyson Cole and Uchi changed all that.

THERE ARE NO boundaries. He likes to blur lines in his dishes.

I WENT FROM FREE labor to his chef de cuisine.

EVERY KITCHEN is different. As long as you accept that there's no right way or wrong way, there's only the chef's way.

WE FOUND our first East Side King truck on someone's lawn on 10th Street. We threw a fryer in there and a fridge and that was it.

WHAT I LOVE about Austin is that everyone is so brave. It's part of that Texas thing. Fuck it. Yeah, I'll do it.

I WASN'T SURE if the whole Top Chef thing was right for me. But I figured there was nothing to lose.

YOU DISAPPEAR for three or four months, and only think about food.

I LIKE all spectrums of food. I'm down to learn the systems of McDonald's, why Chick-fil-A has such a good chicken sandwich.

I TOOK A BIG CHUNK of the Top Chef money and traveled the world, taking notes. —I probably ate at 21 Michelin stars.

A COOK IS in charge of making the food. A chef's job is to inspire people.

WE'RE NOT THAT FAR behind. When I say we, I mean Austin.

WALK-IN'S ONLY. No reservations.

ESSAYS

*Four Austin writers on the far out life of a music legend,
the wonder of natural springs, the city's darkest day
and questions about being homesick at home*

»» THE GROOVE ««

Written by **JOHN SPONG**

THE MOON HUNG FULL, bright and high over the Chihuahuan Desert floor like a bare light bulb illuminating a small-town drunk tank, an observation I'd have been smarter to have considered at the time. I was one of three dudes in a beat up old Land Cruiser, barreling up a West Texas byway at 3:00 A.M. after a long day spent satisfying Texan rites of passage. We'd fed beer to the goat mayor of Lajitas, Clay Henry, that morning; paid fifty cents for a canoe ride twenty feet across the Rio Grande to eat dirty tacos in Old Mexico that afternoon; and then spent the night trading tequila shots with people who live in abandoned mine shafts at both bars in Terlingua. Now we were headed back to a trailer park ten miles away in Study Butte, where our girlfriends had wisely gone to bed hours ago.

The moonlight was sufficient to cast grey shadows off the scattered ocotillo and mesquite scrub, though probably not bright enough for us to be driving without headlights. Still, that's how we'd chosen to make our way, with no regard for cows in the road or the law. Our fate had been placed in the hands of the great Doug Sahm, patron saint of far out trips. If we'd found a tiny alabaster statuette in his likeness—black cowboy hat, long dirty-blond hair, flowing scarf and a duster—we'd have mounted it on the dashboard. But we didn't need that either. We had his CD in the stereo.

The song was a timeless slice of Tex-Mex pop called "Mendocino." It opened with an acoustic guitar strummed in a polka rhythm that seemed to have followed us up from the border. Doug spoke over the intro in a husky drawl. "The Sir Douglas Quintet is back and we'd like to thank all our beautiful friends all over the country for all the beautiful vibrations. We love you." Then Doug started to sing in a soul-shouter's rasp as his lifelong sideman, Augie Meyers, kicked off a bumping organ riff that was sweeter than Big Red.

Teeny Bopper, my teenage lover
I caught your waves last night
It sent my mind to wonderin'.
You're such a groove
Please don't move
Please stay in my love house by the river.

The moment was perfect, the kind that breeds faith that, sometimes, the world really will just get out of your way. When the song ended, we hit it again for the last stretch of the drive, and this time it played out with us parked in front of the trailers. A light came on in a bedroom. Clearly, one of us was headed for hot water. We looked at each other, cracked open another brew, and hit Doug again.

Doug Sahm moved to Austin sometime in or around late 1971 for the stated reason that he was looking for a new groove. In Doug terms, that made perfect sense. All he was ever looking for was one of two things, a hit song or a new groove. The search for the former proved fruitful enough, taking him to the top of the charts and the Grammy winner's podium. But the quest for the latter was more subtle, more challenging. "There's always something trying to disrupt the groove," he used to say in his hopped-up hippie speak. "But the groove's at the center, man. It's the sun. Everything revolves around the groove."

A white-boy son of San Antonio's Eastside neighborhood, he'd picked up the musical styles bouncing around S.A. in the forties—conjunto, blues, and country—and taught himself to play all of them on anything with strings. He was a child prodigy, gigging in country bands around Central Texas before he'd even reached his teens. He was barely eleven when, on December 19, 1952, Hank Williams called him to the stage to play steel with him at the Skyline Club in far North Austin. Two weeks later, when Williams woke up dead in the back of his Cadillac, the Skyline show turned out to have been his final public performance. In Doug lore the night amounted to an anointment.

Through the fifties he recorded country and party rock records with bands like the Mar-Kays and the Pharaohs, but his first real fame came in the sixties as front man and namesake of the Sir Douglas Quintet. That act emphasized the Tex-Mex quotient of his pedigree, most notably in "She's About a Mover," an AM radio hit that peaked at thirteen on the pop charts in 1965. The legend behind the record's creation is almost certainly apocryphal, but also impossible not to repeat: Legendary Houston producer Huey Meaux had grown frustrated with the Beatles taking up all the top spots on the charts, so he'd holed up in a motel room over a weekend with a turntable and their records, intent on cracking the code. He determined that the secret owed in large part to their beat, which he considered a revved-up polka. He relayed this to Doug, and "She's About a Mover" was the the song Doug wrote in response. But Meaux wasn't finished. He sent Doug to tour behind the single under the bogus guise of being a British Invasion band—the Sir Douglas Quintet, get it?—complete with Beatle boots, black suits and mop-top haircuts. Nevermind that three band members were dark-skinned San Antonio Mexicans, or the little likelihood that anyone confused Doug's origins the minute he opened his mouth. "She's About a Mover" was irresistible, a bouncing piece of pop confection that, driven by Augie's roller-rink organ, became a garage rock anthem on par with "Wooly Bully" and "96 Tears."

But while riding that high, Doug got busted with a small amount of pot in Corpus Christi. He split Texas and its hardass drug laws to spend six years in self-imposed exile in San Francisco, getting stoned in Golden Gate Park with the Dead by day and adding psychedelic riffs to his guitar repertoire at the Avalon Ballroom at night. He became buddies with Bob Dylan and scored another Top 40 hit with "Mendocino," then wound up on the cover of Rolling Stone. It was a fertile period; he recorded four albums for Mercury records, two of which—*Mendocino* and *Together After Five*—were among the finest of his career. But the songs he was writing were mostly about Texas. He missed his old friends and his roots. When his marriage started to falter and hard drugs hit the Haight, the scene got too dark for him. Doug split again.

His return to Texas was news enough for *Rolling Stone* to put him on the cover again, this time with the coverline "Sir Douglas Goes Home." The prodigal son was now a bona fide hippie rock star, his hair grown out and a magnificent pair of bushy, porkchop sideburns hanging from under his cowboy hat like fuzzy dice from a low rider's rearview mirror. Visually he was the prototype cosmic cowboy. After a short stay in S.A., where his long hair got his ass kicked by some rednecks outside a taco place, he decided to relocate to Austin.

It wasn't an obvious choice. Austin hadn't established itself as a music town yet, but was better known nationally as the place Janis Joplin had left. Since her departure in 1963, most of the city's younger musicians had followed the national trends, a little folk and a little rock, while the older ones stuck to the traditional Texas strains of country. There was no intermingling; neither camp trusted the other's sound, look, or lifestyle. But just as Doug hit town a group of kids billing themselves as Freda and the Firedogs got a weekly gig at the

A RAMSHACKLE ROAD- HOUSE WEST OF TOWN, SOAP CREEK SALOON WAS THE CENTER OF THE SAHM UNIVERSE.

Split Rail, a country bar just south of the river on Lamar. They were five adventuresome dope-smokers led by a long-legged piano-player named Marcia Ball, and they weren't turned off by straight country music. When Doug stumbled upon their Sunday night residency, he found his new home. Freda played the songs he'd grown up on as a kid. He started sitting in with them at the Split Rail and other spots around town, lending guitar solos that, influenced by his Frisco years, were a little bit longer and a little further out there. Suddenly Austin had its own sound, and its first star.

The most famous venue in town at the time was the Armadillo World Headquarters. Opened in August, 1970, it had quickly become home for the city's counterculture freaks. But it was primarily a concert hall for touring acts; the heart and soul of the burgeoning music scene was Soap Creek Saloon, a ramshackle roadhouse tucked into the cedar breaks some fifteen minutes west of town. The surrounding area was officially called Westlake, and soon enough its dense thickets and high valley vistas would become the preferred destination for well-heeled doctors and lawyers making their mass, white-flight exodus from the city. But at that point its residents were cedar choppers and UT professors, open-minded social outliers who didn't mind the nightly influx of longhairs to the club. Doug felt at ease there too and moved into a two-story stone house on the backside of Soap Creek's dirt parking lot. His old Frisco friends

[*Doug Sahm*]

would crash with him on their way through town, guys like Dylan, the Dead, and Stu and Cosmo from CCR. There were horse stables on one side of the house and raised bait tanks on the other. The landlord, appropriately enough, was a pharmacist.

Soap Creek became the center of the Sahm universe, a summer day-care center for his three young kids, an incubator for new songs he was working up, and a regular stage to play when rent money was due. No fan of telephones, he never installed one at the house, so for quick business like booking local gigs he'd use Soap Creek's payphone. On at least one occasion, his agent, who was in from L.A., accidently left a brown-paper bag containing a few thousand dollars of Doug's cash on a picnic table behind the club. A kindly hippie turned it in at the bar.

But Doug was always hustling, always working an angle, and for bigger business deals he'd drive to friends' houses, from which he'd place surreptitious long-distance calls to his new patrons at Atlantic Records, Jerry Wexler and Ahmet Ertegun. With them he set up the New York sessions that would become 1973's *Doug Sahm* and *Band*, an all-star affair featuring Dylan, Dr. John, and Ray Charles's old sax player, David "Fathead" Newman, backing him up. Doug had high hopes for the record, which jumped from hardcore country to accordion-driven Tex-Mex to faithful renderings of old T-Bone Walker blues shuffles. Eventually it would become like a Rosetta Stone for young Texas musicians trying to reconcile the various strains of their musical heritage. But that status was somewhere off in the future. Atlantic released it but had no idea how to classify it, a confusion the label shared with DJs and record buyers. Commercially, it flopped, Undaunted, Doug returned to Austin and settled back in at Soap Creek, cool in his groove and keeping his eye out for a hit.

I learned a lot of that history as an Austin teenager in the early eighties. Even though those were lean years for Doug, for local kids who spent all their time listening to records and talking about music—kids like me and my friends—his name was inescapable. Our fuller introduction came through a band of his disciples, Joe "King" Carrasco and the Crowns, who'd updated Doug's sound and rebranded it "Nuevo Wavo," then scored a couple minor video hits in the early days of MTV. On Saturdays we liked to go down to campus and swipe beers from college kids we knew, then run around the Drag pulling Joe "King" flyers off phone poles to put up in our bedrooms. Invariably we'd wind up picking through bins at Inner Sanctum Records & Tapes or Aaron's Rock & Roll Emporium, and then bugging the clerks to play Joe "King" records for us. Every time we asked they'd tell us, "Kid, if you like this music, you really need to get some Sir Doug." That was our way in.

But my college years at UT were wasted as far as local music went. I spent my weekends crashing frat parties instead of going to shows, knee-deep in a mainstream country western kick that I think of now—with no remorse—as my George Strait Period. Still, I paid Doug the reverence one of the Austin scene's founding fathers deserved. Occasionally I'd see him in traffic, tooling around town in one of his Cadillacs, and I'd give him a What's-up? head nod. Or on one of the rare occasions I convinced a date to rack out at my place, I'd take her to breakfast the next morning at the Frisco Shop diner, where Doug sat at the counter most mornings, pouring over box scores and flirting with the waitresses. "That's Doug Sahm," I'd whisper. "He's a very important man."

But in the early nineties I started listening to him in present-tense, real time, during his late-career renaissance with the Texas Tornados. They were billed as a Tex-Mex super group featuring better-known names like San Antonio accordionist Flaco Jimenez and South Texas vocalist Freddy Fender, plus Augie and Doug. In Austin, music scene hipsters packed Tornados shows like they'd discovered the hottest new thing, falling for the brown soul vibe and digging on the Tornados' goofy, Spanglish lyrics: "If you've got the dinero/I've got the Camaro." Doug would take the stage like a proper elder statesman, duded up in a brightly colored vest and jacket, with a bolo tie, cowboy hat, dark glasses, and turquoise pinkie ring. And he acted like the attention was long overdue. He wasn't doing anything he hadn't always done. The wider world had simply returned to its senses.

And as I learned more about the band I realized how central to Texas music Doug was. Flaco was the only accordionist most folks had heard of, having backed up acts as varied as Ry Cooder and Dwight Yoakum. But his first exposure outside the Tejano world had been on *Doug Sahm* and *Band* back in 1973. Freddy had been known as the "Mexican Elvis" when he recorded rock songs in Spanish as a teenager in the fifties. But after serving time for a pot bust in the early sixties, he'd disappeared. In 1974, Doug brought him to play Soap Creek and hooked him up with Huey Meaux, who soon had Freddy cut "Before the Next Teardrop Falls." The song became a million-selling, number one single in 1975.

The Tornados had a great run, winning a Grammy for Best Mexican-American Performance in 1990, and having a song penned by Doug, "A Little Bit Is Better Than Nada," play through the opening credits of Kevin Costner's golf movie, *Tin Cup*, in 1996. When they started to slow down in 1997, Doug kept going on his own, performing at small clubs around town like Stubb's inside stage and the Continental Club, and I tried to see him every single time. He'd still keep his band playing long after last call, sometimes going until three in the morning.

But his age was starting to show. At a show at the Hole in the Wall in 1999, he introduced a song with a signature bit of name dropping. "This one's by my old *compadre* Bob Dylan," he said, as the band kicked into a slow, bluesy vamp. Knowing he'd never remember the cryptic lyrics on his own, he'd placed a Dylan songbook on a music stand next to the microphone. It was thick as a phone book. And even though Doug had his reading glasses on, he couldn't find the song. While the band kept playing, he scanned the table of contents, flipped to the index, and then just started turning pages. He searched for a good ten minutes and never did find it. No matter. With the band still going, he stifled a giggle, nailed a couple Freddy King licks to segue into another number, and stepped back to the mic. "Here's a hit by my old friend, Roky Erickson," he said. "Roky, this one's for you, brother. It's called 'You're Gonna Miss Me.'" The crowd erupted like Roky had just entered the club with Dylan on his shoulders.

That ended up being the last Doug show I ever saw. A few months later, in November, Doug bolted on one of his frequent, spur of the moment roadtrips, this one to New Mexico. The newspaper would later report that he'd called his son on his way out of town to let him know he was leaving and casually mentioned he was suffering a little indigestion. But later that night, at a Taos motel called the Thunderbird, he had a heart attack and died. He was just fifty-eight.

Word spread through Austin the next afternoon, and that

night we three buddies of the West Texas road trip assembled to pay our respects. We made stops by Antone's and the Continental, the two clubs where we'd seen Doug play the most often. But their scenes were too somber, and we knew that a random, previously-booked band doing a couple Doug covers wasn't going to take us where we needed to go. We hopped into that same old Land Cruiser and started to drive. We played some Tornados, then ventured back in time to "Mendocino" and "Nuevo Laredo" and "She's About a Mover." Finally we landed on "At the Crossroads," one of the songs Doug had written while he was out in California and pining for Texas. "You can teach me lots of lesson, you can bring me lots of gold," he sang. "But you just can't live in Texas if you don't have a lot of soul."

JOHN SPONG is a senior editor at Texas Monthly, where he's been a finalist for a National Magazine Award and has twice won the Texas Institute of Letters' O. Henry Award for Magazine Journalism.

≫ WATERS ≪

Written by **JOE NICK PATOSKI**

1963. *Aquarena Springs, San Marcos, Texas.*

I'm twelve years old, riding in the back seat of my father's Studebaker Silver Hawk next to my older sister. My father steers us south from Fort Worth towards South Padre Island for our summer vacation. It's a long, all-day drive on mostly two-lane highways filled with boredom, but my sister and I have whined enough to persuade the old man to follow the billboards to Aquarena, a genuine roadside attraction just south of Austin.

We want to see Ralph the Swimming Pig do his Swine Dive. We want to watch the aquamaids and Glurpo the Clown perform in the Submarine Theatre, just like the billboards have been promising for the past hundred miles. But before we go, we take a ride across Spring Lake in a glass-bottom boat, a rather lame means of transport, done in the tradition of Weeki Wachee Springs in Florida. Spring Lake is the dammed up portion of San Marcos Springs, the second biggest springs complex in the southwestern part of America. They tell us that humans have lived here for over 14,000 years.

I've never seen water like this. It startles me. Back in Fort Worth, the Trinity River cuts through the city, wide and muddy, a tree-tangled drainage. The water at Aquarena is clear, inviting, perfect. I feel like I'm far away from Texas.

The Submarine Theatre is sort of corny but does not disappoint. The viewing area submerges below for an underwater view of the lake. Ralph dives dramatically, several times. Pigs are very good swimmers, especially when enticed by a swimmer holding a baby bottle. Glurpo gets some laughs drinking Dr Pepper while underwater. The come-hither aquamaids enjoy a picnic lunch while breathing through air hoses.

Back on land, we put enough coins into a machine to compel a chicken to play basketball by pecking at a string and launching a toy ball towards a small hoop. Our father nixes a Skyride and a trip up the observation tower. It's back to the car. The beach is still almost 400 miles away.

1974. *Barton Springs, Austin, Texas.*

It's a hot afternoon in June. I'm a budding rock critic, but I drive cabs and clerk in record stores to support my habit and the late nights I spend at the Armadillo World Headquarters and Soap Creek Saloon. I stand at the edge of Barton Springs. My girlfriend coaxes me to swim across the width of the pool. I am wary. The water temperature is sixty-eight degrees. Icewater. Cold enough to trigger a flashback of sticking an arm into the bin of watermelons floating in a tub of ice at Buddies grocery, holding it in until it hurt too much.

"C'mon," she says.

My motivation is the instant shock of chill when I hit the water; I'll swim fast, so I can get out of the water and back into the sun.

But when I open my eyes underwater and look below, I can't help but slow down. The water is transparent and there is so much to see. My eyes don't sting when I open them. No chlorine, just freshwater in its most natural state. From below, I watch a duck paddle its feet and I realize how perfect waterfowl are designed. A red-eared slider turtle zips along effortlessly. A couple large bass hang in lush aquatic vegetation, seamlessly blending into the background.

OUR CAR SLOWLY CRAWLS ACROSS A LOW-WATER CROSSING OVER THE BLANCO RIVER, THROUGH A FOOT OF MOVING WATER.

I will swim a mile almost every day during the summer [becoming very cranky on days I that I don't]. I'm hooked so bad that my swimming season stretches into pleasant days during the fall and spring. Even the winter. On chillier days, the sixty-eight degree water actually feels warm, as long as I get moving. It becomes my place. On the January day that Prince Charles visually inspects Barton, the high temperature hits ninety degrees and hundreds of swimmers and sunbathers are in and around the pool. On the hot August morning when others share the pool with the entire Dallas Cowboys football squad, sixty-eight degrees is chilly enough to make 300-pound lineman squeal like a baby.

I stand at the shallow end and look downstream to the walled end of the pool, where the water tumbles into Barton Creek, a few hundred yards from Town Lake. The downtown skyline peeks above the green wall of oak and pecan trees, a mile across the river.

I read up on Juan Ponce de Leon, wondering if he had been a thousand miles off course. I can't help but think about the native tribes and early settlers who witnessed this creek long before I do. It is a ribbon of cool spring-fed water that begins underground forty miles upstream, twisting and writhing between steep limestone cliffs on its course towards the heart of the city.

They must have thought they'd stumbled into Paradise.

1993. *The Blanco River, seven miles upstream from the village of Wimberley. Hays County.*

The afternoon is sticky humid hot, like a damp heated blanket has covered my entire being. It'll be like this until September. The wife and I are returning from a pleasant weekend on a houseboat on Lake Amistad, a dammed up part of the Rio Grande in southwest Texas. We are about to look at a house she's found in the Hill Country for our family. I had suggested she look for a place with a swimming hole, since we can't afford to move next to Barton Springs. This place has river access.

Our car slowly crawls across a low-water crossing over the Blanco River, through a foot of moving water. We glance upstream as we nervously cross the river. The rushing water swishes under our tires. There are people standing in shallow water. A few appear to be swimming. Three float in inner tubes. I tell my wife I'm sold, even though we haven't seen the house yet. It does not hurt that as we turn up the caliche road to our future home, a nine-banded armadillo scurries from below a spreading oak at least three hundred years old. I am home.

fig.1 BARTON SPRINGS

1999. *Aquarena Springs, San Marcos, Texas.*

I'm back at Aquarena, only it isn't Aquarena anymore. The roadside attraction has closed, done in by newer shinier destinations. Six Flags Fiesta Texas, Sea World, a waterpark twenty miles away called Schlitterbahn. Aquarena has been purchased by Texas State University. All the swimming pigs that performed as Ralph have been semi-retired to their trainer's home on Lime Kiln Road, and the site will be dedicated to researching the springs.

I'm doing a short story on the transition for Texas Monthly magazine, where I am a staff writer. I invoke journalist privilege to ask if I can swim where Ralph and Glurpo once swam. It's now the exclusive domain of archeological divers.

It takes several requests. And once I'm given permission, there's a kicker: I'm to be followed by a glass-bottom boat. Still, I immediately get lost once underwater. It's clearer than any water I've swum in the Caribbean over the past twenty years, visibility sharp, all the way to the bottom twenty-five feet below. I steadily stroke and kick, and I suddenly recognize Cream of Wheat Springs.

2013. *The Blanco River, seven miles upstream of the village of Wimberley, Hays County.*

On a sunny Saturday in late March, I finally get in and swim a short lap in the river. First swim of the year. The surrounding grasses are still bleached winter white and weather conditions remain awfully dry. The river is in sore need of a big flood to flush out the channel and scour the limestone bottom, now coated with a thick, muddy layer of fresh sediment. The weakened springs need some energy.

No rain. This continuation of a three-year drought [or ten-year, depending who you talk to] could permanently alter what I'm looking at.

No rain. I start wondering how soon will the day arrive when the whole region will go Mars on me and leave behind an empty channel of sun-bleached white limestock rocks?

But with the air temperature in the high eighties, the cypress trees producing green shoots, and the birds making a beautiful racket with their early spring songs, I cannot resist. I only do a half lap to the low water crossing. The dog jumps in and swims alongside, a habit he developed last summer. No rain and I won't be swimming this August. But I can only fret so much. The clarity of this part of the Blanco is nowhere near that of Barton Springs or San Marcos Springs. But the feel and taste of cool, clean Hill Country spring water more than compensates. The water remains irresistible.

2013. *Barton Springs, Austin, Texas.*

I return to Barton Springs, sporadically. My sons both live in Austin now. They are regulars at Barton. Both received Barton baptisms before they could walk. It's in their DNA. I've been gone long enough to notice changes at Barton Springs. There is new vegetation in the men's bathhouse to keep company with the grand old banana plant by the shower. The new personnel collects my admission fee. But really, the cosmetic changes do not touch the timelessness of the place. That simple pleasure of gliding through cold spring water, lifting my head while doing laps to make out newer, taller skyscrapers rising above the wall of green. For all the other visible changes, the underwater scene through my goggles remains. I dip my head into that chilly water. It's that same blue-and-green tinted world. It fills me with wonder, for as long as I can hold my breath.

JOE NICK PATOSKI spent 18 years as a staff writer for *Texas Monthly*, and has also authored biographies of Willie Nelson, Selena, and Stevie Ray Vaughan. He lives near the Blanco River in Wimberley, Texas.

⫸ 96 MINUTES ⫷

Written by **PAMELA COLLOFF** | **ON THE MORNING** of August 1, 1966, not long before classes at the University of Texas at Austin were about to let out for lunch, an architectural engineering major named Charles Whitman arrived at the Tower dressed as a maintenance man. He would be described the following day in the Austin American as "a good son, an excellent Marine, an honor student, a loving husband, a handsome man, a wonderful friend—and an expert sniper." The footlocker he wheeled behind him contained three rifles, two pistols, and a sawed-off shotgun, as well as canned peaches, deodorant, an alarm clock, binoculars, toilet paper, a machete, and sweet rolls. After a receptionist switched on an elevator that Whitman had been trying in vain to operate, he smiled and said, "Thank you, ma'am. You don't know how happy that makes me."

Whitman rode the elevator to the twenty-seventh floor, dragged his footlocker up the stairs to the observation deck, and introduced the nation to the idea of mass murder in a public space. Before 9/11, before Columbine, before the Oklahoma City bombing, the 25-year-old ushered in the notion that any group of people, anywhere—even walking around a university campus—could be killed at random by a stranger. Hundreds of students, professors, tourists, and store clerks witnessed the 96-minute killing spree as they crouched behind trees, hid under desks, took cover in stairwells, or, if they had been hit, played dead.

Both the Associated Press and United Press International would rank the shootings as the second most important story of the year, behind only the war in Vietnam. But until 1999, when the university dedicated a memorial garden near the Tower to the victims, no plaques had ever been displayed, no list of names read, no memorial services held. Decades of institutional silence had turned the shootings, and Whitman himself, into the answers to trivia questions. But, of course, there was nothing at all trivial about that day.

Whitman's first shot was fired at 11:48 a.m.

SHELTON WILLIAMS *was a senior at UT. He is the President of the Osgood Center for International Studies, in Washington, D.C.* It was a few minutes to noon, and I was driving down the Drag in my brand-new red 1966 Mustang. It was a bright, sunshiny day. I remember "Monday, Monday," by the Mamas and the Papas, playing on the radio. We got to the stoplight that's right there outside of the University Co-op Bookstore, and that's when I heard it. A lot of people thought it was a car backfiring or a sound they just couldn't discern. I attribute this to the fact that I'm from West Texas, but I knew immediately that it was gunshots.

JOHN PIPKIN *was a senior. He is a retired money manager in Houston.* A couple of buddies and I had gone down to Scholz Garten. We were eating sandwiches when some guy busts open the door and jumps up on the bar and starts screaming for everybody's attention. He's yelling, "You gotta hear what I'm saying! There's a sniper up on the Tower and he's shooting people!" Everybody in the place starts laughing and saying, "Yeah, right—a sniper on the Tower. Let's drink to the sniper!" So everybody raises their beers and makes a big joke out of it. And about that time, we started to hear sirens.

BRENDA BELL *was a junior. She is a reporter at the Austin American-Statesman.* Random violence and mass murder wasn't something we knew. We had no reference point then. We weren't even scared at first. We were just wildly curious. I was in Shakespeare class when it started, and we all ran to the windows of the English building, which is now Parlin Hall, and stood there peering out over each other's shoulders.

CLAIRE JAMES *was a freshman. She teaches elementary and junior high school in Tucson, Arizona.* My boyfriend, Tom Eckman, and I were walking across the South Mall, holding hands, when all of a sudden I felt like I'd stepped on a live wire, like I'd been electrocuted. I was eight months pregnant at the time. Tom said, "Baby—" and reached out for me. And then he was hit.

MICHAEL HALL *was a history professor. Now retired, he lives in Austin.* There was a loud crack outside Garrison Hall. I went outside to see what was going on, and I saw a body lying there on the cement in the middle of the mall, in the very bright sunlight. To my left, there were three live oak trees, magnificent specimens with very large trunks. A young man was crouched down behind one of them, his fingertips touching the bark, terrified, staring up at the Tower.

DAVID BAYLESS JR. *was a freshman. He sells insurance in Denison.* People started pouring out of classrooms; it was lunchtime and everyone was in a hurry. I held my arms out and tried to block the doors that led out onto the South Mall. I said, "Don't go out there. Someone's shooting people." But no one believed me. They looked at me like I was a dumb kid and pushed right past.

CLAIRE JAMES: Tom never said another word. I was lying next to him on the pavement, and I called out to him, but I knew he was dead. A conservative-looking guy in a suit walked by, and I yelled at him, "Please, get a doctor! Please!" He looked annoyed and said, "Get up! What do you think you're doing?" I think he thought it was guerrilla theater, because we had started doing things like that to bring attention to the war in Vietnam.

BOB HIGLEY *was a junior. He is the managing director of an investment firm in Houston.* To me, the university had always seemed like an idyllic place. It was devoted to ideas and learning. It was shocking to me that one person, a fellow student, could ruin all that so quickly. He was killing indiscriminately, aiming wherever he saw targets—riding their bicycles, looking out windows, walking down the Drag.

GAYLE ROSS *was a junior. She is records supervisor at the Plano Police Department.* I knew this was no ordinary day. It had that same feeling of time isolated, before and after, that the Kennedy assassination had. Normal life had stopped, and for this little space of time, everything revolved around the Tower and that man.

By three o'clock on the morning of the shootings, Whitman had stabbed and strangled his mother, Margaret, in her apartment and stabbed his wife, Kathy, in their bed. In the half-typed, half-handwritten letter he left on Kathy's body, he wrote, "Lately [I can't recall when it started] I have been a victim of many unusual and irrational thoughts … I have been fighting my mental turmoil alone, and seemingly to no avail. After my death I wish that an autopsy would be performed on me to see if there is any visible physical disorder … Maybe research can prevent further tragedies of this type."

DAVE MCNEELY *was a reporter in the Houston Chronicle's Capitol bureau. He is a syndicated newspaper columnist in Austin.* I met Charles Whitman that summer at his birthday party. Whitman was blond, good-looking, solidly built. I remember he seemed like a nice, clean-cut, all-American kind of guy.

BARTON RILEY *was an instructor in architectural engineering. A retired architect, he lives in Kerrville.* Charlie was one of my students. He didn't have many friends. From what I understood, his father was a rather crude man and had kicked him around a bit. When he came to the university, he wanted to excel; he wanted to show his father up.

> **WE WALKED OUT ONTO THE OBSERVATION DECK, LOOKING DOWN AT THE WHOLE CITY. IT JUST WENT ON AND ON, AND IT WAS SO BEAUTIFUL.**

SHELTON WILLIAMS: Charlie always chewed on his fingernails while he read over his notes. I'd never seen anyone work so vigorously on their fingernails; I couldn't believe there was anything left to chew. I remember a kid walked up to him once and said, "Say, Charlie, are you going to go to Vietnam and kill Charlie?" The kid thought that was hilarious. Whitman said, "The Marines can kiss my red-white-and-blue ass."

BARTON RILEY: Charlie called me at eleven o'clock one night and said, "I need to see you." I said, "Now?" and he said yes. So I turned the porch light on and waited for him. He was very flushed when he walked in the door, but the moment he saw that I had a baby grand in my living room, he sat down and played "Claire de Lune." He did it beautifully. When all that red had drained out of his face, he stood up and left.

GARY LAVERGNE *is the author of A Sniper in the Tower: The Charles*

Whitman Murders. In early September of 1961 Whitman was standing on the seventh-floor balcony of his dorm, looking at the Tower, when he turned to a friend and said, "You know, that would be a great place to go up with a rifle and shoot people. You could hold off an army for as long as you wanted." Instead of seeing the Tower, he saw a fortress. It never occurred to his friend that he might be serious.

The day before the shootings, a teenager from Rockdale named Cheryl Botts [now Cheryl Dickerson] came to Austin to visit her grandmother. When she arrived, she met UT student Don Walden, and he offered to show her around campus the next day on his motorcycle. They arrived at the Tower the following morning, not long before Whitman took control of the observation deck. The Gabours, a family visiting from Texarkana, arrived soon after.

CHERYL DICKERSON *was a freshman at Howard Payne University, in Brownwood. She is a textbook consultant in Luling.* We walked out onto the observation deck, looking down at the whole city. I grew up in a very small town, so the thing that impressed me was how big everything was. I mean, it just went on and on, and it was so beautiful.

DAVID MATTSON *was a Peace Corps trainee living in Austin. A retired teacher, he lives in Hastings, Minnesota.* I'm reminded of the article that was in Time magazine a week or two later that compared the shootings to Thornton Wilder's novel *The Bridge of San Luis Rey.* In the book, people from all walks of life were, for various reasons, drawn together by fate to a critical time and place in space. Everyone was there for a different reason when the bridge, which spans a gorge in Peru, collapses and they fall to their deaths.

CHERYL DICKERSON: We stepped back inside, and I noticed that the receptionist was not at her desk, but I just assumed she had gone to lunch. The next thing I saw was this reddish-brown swath that we had to step over. My instinct was that someone was about to varnish the floor. Immediately to our right, a blond guy stood up. We had surprised him, apparently. He was bending over the couch, and we found out later that he had put the receptionist's body there. He turned around to face us, and he had a rifle in each hand. Don thought—I know this sounds crazy—that he was there to shoot pigeons. So I smiled at him and said, "Hello," and he smiled back at me and said, "Hi." I figured out later when I read the newspaper that while we were going down in one elevator, the Gabours must have been coming up in the other.

MICHAEL GABOUR *was a cadet at the U.S. Air Force Academy, in Colorado Springs, Colorado. He owns a radio station in Port Douglas, Australia.* After getting off the elevator, we began the climb to the observation deck. My brother, my aunt, and my mother followed slightly farther behind. As I reached the top of the stairs, I saw a pretty-good-sized blond dude wearing aviator shades running toward me. The barrel of what looked like a sawed-off automatic twelve-gauge shotgun was coming up to firing position. I had just started to turn toward my family when the first blast caught my left shoulder. I'm not sure if it was that round, or one of the many subsequent ones, that killed my brother and my aunt.

HERB RITCHIE *was a sophomore. He is a former judge in Houston.* I was in the classics department, on the highest floor of the Tower. There was a really loud noise that sounded like filing cabinets had fallen down the stairs. Professor Mench came running and said, "There are bodies in the stairwell."

MICHAEL GABOUR: My father tried to pull me down the blood-filled hallway. I told him to go for help, and he did.

HERB RITCHIE: We barricaded ourselves inside an office. I put a rolling blackboard up against the door. There were about eight of us, including two nuns. One of the sisters talked about the poor, twisted soul up there who was shooting people. I didn't have much sympathy at all.

In the first few minutes of Whitman's killing spree, many students were unaware of what was happening; some thought it was the work of drama students or an experiment being performed by the psychology department or just a joke. Victims lay where they had fallen on the hot cement and tried to play dead. But Whitman never shot again once he had hit his target. In the sniper tradition of "one shot, one kill," he never wasted a bullet on someone who was down.

CLAIRE JAMES: I didn't know it at the time, but I was losing a lot of blood; I felt like I was melting. The pavement was so hot that it was burning the backs of my legs.

DAVID MATTSON: I was walking with two other Peace Corps volunteers down the Drag; we were headed to Sheftall's jewelers, because I needed to get my watch fixed. I was showing my friends my watch, when all of a sudden my hand came crashing down and, when I looked down, I saw that part of my wrist had been blown away. The manager inside Sheftall's pulled us into the store.

ANN MAJOR *was a senior. She is a romance novelist living in Corpus Christi.* I went down to the basement of Parlin Hall and listened to the radio. I remember hearing the radio announcer say he had shot a boy off his bicycle near the Night Hawk restaurant, several blocks away.

KAY BAILEY HUTCHISON *was a law student. She is the former U.S. senator from Texas.* I was in class when the shooting began. We could see the smoke from the gun each time it fired, although we did not know at the time that he was marking innocent people.

BILL HELMER *was a graduate student in American history. He is a historical-crime writer living in Boerne.* I was more or less marveling at this nut on the Tower until a shot came in through the open window and hit the arm of the guy beside me. Then I got a wee bit rattled. I thought, "Son of a bitch! This guy is good."

JOHN PIPKIN: I heard about a guy who was eating a sandwich in the front yard of the Kappa house, minding his own business, when he was shot through the chest.

GARY LAVERGNE: The farthest casualty was well over five hundred yards away, at the A&E Barber Shop, on the Drag. A basketball coach named Billy Snowden got out of the barber's chair to get a better look. He was standing in the doorway, with his smock still on, when he was shot in the shoulder.

CLAIRE JAMES: A really lovely young woman with red hair ran up to me and said, "Please, let me help you." I told her to get down so she wouldn't attract attention, and she lay down next to me. It was

[*UT Tower*]

a beautiful, selfless act. I told her my name and my blood type, and she made sure to keep me talking so I wouldn't lose consciousness. She stayed with me for at least an hour, until people came and carried me away.

DAVID MATTSON: A policeman finally pounded on the back door and said, "There's an ambulance just a couple of doors down." By the time we got to the ambulance, the driver had been shot. He was laid out in the back. We squeezed in beside him, and the policeman took us to the hospital, driving down alleys and using buildings for cover.

ROBERT HEARD *was a reporter for the Associated Press.* Ernie Stromberger, of the Dallas Times Herald, and I drove to campus and parked behind two highway patrolmen. When they ran across Twenty-fourth Street, Ernie stayed put; I followed, a few seconds behind them. Just before I reached the curb, I was shot down. I'd forgotten my Marine training; I hadn't zigzagged. It felt like someone had hit my shoulder with a brick.

JOHN ECONOMIDY *was a senior and the editor of the Daily Texan.* I took off for the Texan. When I ran into the newsroom, I saw a couple of my photographers just standing there, looking through the venetian blinds. I said, "Get off your butts. Get out there and win the Pulitzer Prize!"

ROBERT HEARD: A group of students—I never knew who they were—ran out into the street, knowing they could be shot, and dragged me under the trunk of a Studebaker. Ernie Stromberger called in to the Times Herald and said, "Tell the people at the AP that they no longer have a man on the job."

HARPER SCOTT CLARK *was a junior. A veteran journalist, he lives in Killeen.* I went to Scholz's at around 12:10, and it was packed. There was a businessman standing near me—your typical good old boy in cowboy boots and pressed jeans and Western-style shirt—and he said, "Well, I hope they get him off that Tower pretty quick, because the anti-gun people are going to go crazy over this."

Students waited and waited for the police to arrive. The Austin Police

Department had no tactical unit to deploy. Its officers had only service revolvers and shotguns, which were useless against a sniper whose perch was hundreds of yards away. The phones system was jammed across the city. In the absence of any visible police presence, students decided to defend themselves.

JAMES DAMON *was a graduate student in comparative literature. A retired real estate investor, he lives in Austin.* My wife was six months pregnant, and she was stuck on the fourth floor of the Tower. I looked around and didn't see any police, so I went home and got my gun. It was an M1 carbine. I went to the top of the new Academic Center and tried to keep out of sight. From time to time I would shoot over the ledge of the observation deck and try to hit him.

CLIF DRUMMOND *was a senior and the student body president. He is a high-tech executive in Austin.* Students with deer rifles were leaning up against telephone poles, using the pole, which is rather narrow, as their shield. And they were firing like crazy back at the Tower.

FORREST PREECE *was a junior. A retired advertising executive, he lives in Austin.* I saw two guys in white shirts and slacks running across the lawn of the Pi Phi house, hustling up to its porch with rifles at the ready. Someone was yelling, "Keep down, man. Keep down!"

J. M. COETZEE *was a Ph.D. candidate in English literature and linguistics. A novelist who won the 2003 Nobel Prize for literature, he lives in Adelaide, Australia.* I hadn't fully comprehended that lots of people around me in Austin not only owned guns but had them close at hand and regarded themselves as free to use them.

BILL HELMER: I remember thinking, "All we need is a bunch of idiots running around with rifles." But what they did turned out to be brilliant. Once he could no longer lean over the edge and fire, he was much more limited in what he could do. That's why he did most of his damage in the first twenty minutes.

JOHN PIPKIN: I'd left Scholz's and was sitting across the street from the Chi Omega house when this Texas Ranger walked up carrying a pair of binoculars and a rifle with a scope on it. For some reason, he picked me out of the group of kids and said, "Son, you ever done any hunting?" And I said, "Yes, sir, I've been hunting all my life." He said, "Well, take these binoculars. I need for you to calibrate me." Whitman would stick his rifle out through one of these drainpipes every once in a while and shoot at someone. The ranger would shoot back, and I'd say, "You're an inch too high," or "Bring it over to the left a couple inches."

BRENDA BELL: I don't know where these vigilantes came from, but they took over Parlin Hall and were crashing around, firing guns. There was massive testosterone.

JOHN PIPKIN: All of a sudden I thought to myself, "Gosh, he's pointing that rifle at me." It was like I could see up inside the barrel of the rifle. The next thing I knew, I could feel bullets grazing the top of the hair on my head. The ranger said, "Boy, we got his attention now." I was absolutely terrified.

BOB HIGLEY: Across the street was a student sitting against a parking meter, obviously wounded, his head slumped over. Clif Drummond and I later learned his name was Paul Sonntag. Drummond said something and we looked each other in the eye and had a Butch Cassidy and the Sundance Kid kind of moment. I said, "Are you going first or am I?"

CLIF DRUMMOND: There was essentially abject silence except for the sound of the shooting echoing off the limestone. Cars were sitting out in the middle of the Drag with their doors hanging open, motors running, no one in them.

BOB HIGLEY: Drummond led out. I went one or two steps behind him, and if he moved left, I moved more to the right, and we went straight across the Drag.

CLIF DRUMMOND: We got shot at as we crossed the street, but he missed. I remember the pavement flicking, bursting, as bullets were hitting it.

BOB HIGLEY: We worked our way up, on our bellies, to Sonntag. Drummond felt for a pulse and couldn't find one. Sonntag's fingers were totally blue. That's when I saw he had been hit right in the mouth. He must have heard the gunshot and turned to look over his shoulder at the Tower.

CLIF DRUMMOND: A person we didn't know in a station wagon—someone crazier than us—came wheeling around Twenty-fourth Street and roared to a stop in front of us. The cognition kicked in right then, and I remember thinking to myself, "This is really damned serious."

BOB HIGLEY: We were sitting ducks. It was right then that my fear gave way to anger, just pure anger. I was still thinking that Sonntag had been badly wounded. I couldn't allow myself to believe that this kid was dead.

NEAL SPELCE *was the news director for KTBC-TV. A retired anchorman, he lives in Spicewood.* Our radio news director, Joe Roddy, went to Brackenridge Hospital and read the names off the first list of casualties. As soon as he finished, Paul Bolton grabbed the microphone and said, "Joe, hold it." Bolton was the very first television news anchor in Austin, a good friend of LBJ's. He was a gruff, hard-boiled newsman, but you could hear that his voice was wavering. He said, "I think you have my grandson on there. Go over that list of names again, please." Well, his grandson was Paul Sonntag. His full name, we later found out, was Paul Bolton Sonntag——his namesake. Joe read through the list again, and Bolton pretty much broke down in the newsroom.

Thirty-nine of Whitman's victims were taken to the emergency room of Brackenridge Hospital in the span of ninety minutes. The first victim arrived at 12:12 p.m., and patients continued arriving at the rate of one every two minutes for the first hour.

CAMILLE CLAY *was a nursing supervisor at Brackenridge. Now retired, she lives in Austin.* The emergency room looked like something you'd see in Vietnam. I had never seen anything like it in my life.

HOWARD HUGHES *was an intern at the hospital. He is a physician at the University of Texas Health Center in Austin.* Many of the wounds were bleeding out quickly, so we shouted back and forth, trying to decide which patients should go to the operating rooms first. There was blood everywhere.

PATSY GERMAN *was a graduate student in history. A retired teacher, she lives in Richardson.* I remember the nauseating feeling when they kept reporting the death toll on TV. We all went to the blood bank near Brackenridge, and the lines of cars went on for what seemed like miles.

HOWARD HUGHES: Many of the victims seemed to have well-placed shots through the chest, with the exception of the pregnant lady, who was shot in the abdomen.

CLAIRE JAMES: I knew immediately that I'd lost the baby. By the eighth month, your baby's moving a lot. And after I got shot, the baby never moved.

CAMILLE CLAY: We put the victims who we believed to be deceased in one room. You just couldn't believe it, all those dead teenagers lying on the floor. We started trying to identify them. One in particular I remember was a boy who was wearing a class ring from Austin High School that was engraved with his initials. I called the principal and asked him to pull the records for the class of 1966.

Police officer Ramiro Martinez was at home, off duty, and cooking himself a steak for lunch when he saw KTBC's noon news bulletin. Martinez put on his uniform, jumped in his 1954 Chevrolet, and drove to campus. When he saw that there were more than enough officers directing traffic away from the university, he decided to head for the Tower.

RAMIRO MARTINEZ *was a patrolman for the Austin Police Department. A retired Texas Ranger, he lives in New Braunfels.* When I reached the South Mall, I could see people hiding behind trees and hedges. There was a pregnant woman who was twisting, wilting, in the hot sun. I ran as fast as I could, zigzagging toward the Tower, and somehow made it without getting shot.

I couldn't make contact with the department. I tried the phone, but the lines were jammed. At that point, I decided that I needed to get upstairs.

I got on the elevator and pressed the button for the twenty-seventh floor. By that time I was starting to feel pretty uneasy, so as I was going up in the elevator, watching those little numbers light up, I decided to say an Act of Contrition. Then I pulled out my .38 and pointed it at the elevator doors. I didn't know what I was going to find when I got to the top of the Tower.

When the elevator doors opened, police officer Jerry Day and a civilian named Allen Crum were facing me holding a pistol and a rifle. We all let out huge sighs of relief. An officer with the Department of Public Safety was sitting at a desk, dialing, trying to establish communications. The man next to him was drawing a map of the observation deck— and that was it. There was no game plan. We were the whole enchilada.

I had started opening doors when I saw a very distraught middle-aged man holding a pair of white women's shoes with blood on them. He was M. J. Gabour [Michael's father]. He said, "The son of a bitch killed my family up there. Let me have your gun and I'll go kill him." He tried to grab my gun away from me, so we wrestled him into the elevator, and Day took him downstairs.

Finally, I opened the door that led up to the observation deck. There were bloody footprints on the stairs. Knowing I had to walk up those steps was a lonely feeling. Allen Crum said, "Where are you going?" I said, "Up." He said, "Well, I'm coming with you."

When we reached the first landing, I could see the face of a young boy. His eyes were open, looking at me, and he was dead. There was a wounded young man who was slumped against a wall, still conscious. He said, "He's outside," and pointed upstairs.

The shooting outside sounded just like rolling thunder. There were shell casings everywhere. Crum kept me covered while I looked around the southeast corner, but the sniper was not in sight. I kept down, because the bullets that civilians were firing from down below kept hitting the limestone and showering dust and little pieces of rock.

Before I reached the northeast corner, I turned and saw an officer I knew, Houston McCoy, standing behind me with a shotgun. I advanced to the northeast corner, looked around it, and that's when I saw the sniper. He was sitting about forty feet away with an M1 carbine, and he looked like he had a target in his sights. I immediately fired a round at him and hit him somewhere on his left side. He leapt to his feet and started to turn around, trying to bring his rifle down to return fire. I emptied my gun. I hollered at McCoy to fire, which he did, hitting him. The sniper started going down, and that's when I reached up—my gun was empty—and grabbed the shotgun from McCoy. I blasted him one more time as he was falling. And then it was over.

The shooting ended at 1:24 p.m. Allen Crum found a towel and waved it over his head to signal that the ordeal was over. All told, Whitman had shot 43 people. Fifteen were dead, including his wife and his mother.

ANN MAJOR: Everybody poured out of their hiding places. It was a beautiful, sunny day, but I saw many dead people, mostly young, lying on the grass where they had been shot. I remember hearing the chilling sound of what surely was every siren on every ambulance in Austin.

JOHN PIPKIN: The world came alive again. Hundreds of people emerged from wherever they had been hiding. The Tower was like a magnet; everyone started walking toward it.

FORREST PREECE: I was part of a huge mass of people sweeping east toward the Tower. The whole crowd was silent. A weird tableau of three men walking west parted us like the Red Sea. I instantly knew who they were and what they had done. In the middle was a Hispanic police

I TRIED THE PHONE, BUT THE LINES WERE JAMMED. AT THAT POINT, I DECIDED THAT I NEEDED TO GET UPSTAIRS.

officer who seemed to be in a state of shock. His uniform was soaked through. His eyes were locked into the thousand-yard stare. The man on his left was whispering soothing words to him as they walked past: "You did okay, buddy. Ease up. You did okay. It's all right."

CLIF DRUMMOND: I had never seen that many people crammed into such a small space. I want to say there were easily a thousand people standing shoulder to shoulder. There wasn't a breeze moving in any direction, and the crowd was totally quiet. There were lots of rifles. You could see the barrels sticking up out of the crowd.

BILL HELMER: The cops took fifteen or twenty minutes. They wheeled Whitman out on a stretcher——out the back, to avoid the mob. He was all shot to hell.

BRENDA BELL: There was blood everywhere. It was hot, so it had turned dark. It was on the mall, all over the sidewalk, up and down the Drag, on the carpet of Sheftall's jewelers. But it was all cleaned up very fast. One of the orders that [UT regent] Frank Erwin gave was "Clean this mess up."

SHEL HERSHORN *was a photographer for Life magazine. He died in* 2011. I'd gotten a call in Dallas from Life telling me to get down to Austin. By the time I got there, Whitman was dead. I'd heard there was a foot-wide swath of blood across the carpet at Sheftall's, so I went there and started making pictures. One of those pictures ended up being the cover photo for the magazine; it was taken through the store window, which was shot up with bullet holes. But this competing photographer was pacing up and down the sidewalk outside, waiting his turn. So when I was done, I kicked the window out. I said, "Life magazine will pay for that."

When an autopsy was performed on Whitman the next morning, Dr. Coleman de Chenar discovered what appeared to be a small brain tumor. The consensus in the medical community, however, was that the tumor was probably not to blame, given its size and location. [Whitman was not neurologically impaired at the time of the shootings, for example; he was a crack shot.]

JOHN ECONOMIDY: It turned out that Whitman had gone into the Student Health Center that spring complaining of terrible headaches and depression and had seen a psychiatrist named Maurice Heatly. Whitman had told him exactly what he planned to do. Heatly wrote in his report, which was released to reporters, that Whitman was "oozing with hostility" and had expressed a desire to go to the top of the Tower and shoot people with a deer rifle.

SHELTON WILLIAMS: The cover of Life the next week made a big impression on all of us. From that vantage point the Tower looked menacing, even evil—not the triumphant symbol of football victories we were used to.

FORREST PREECE: I was sitting with the rest of the Longhorn Band in Memorial Stadium at the first football game that September. I remember that John Wayne was in attendance.

BARTON RILEY: The fall semester started and I never heard it mentioned. Isn't that amazing?

CLAIRE JAMES: I was in intensive care for seven weeks. I had to learn how to walk again. When I went back to school in January, no one said anything to me or talked about it around me. If it was mentioned at all, it was always called "the accident."

The observation deck was closed after the shootings and then reopened two years later. The board of regents closed it indefinitely in 1974, after a series of suicides. It reopened on September 16, 1999.

HARPER SCOTT CLARK: A bullet of Whitman's had ripped a big chunk out of one of the balustrades on the South Mall, and whenever my friends and I would stroll by there, we would run our fingers inside it. I went back years later and saw that someone had filled it in with plaster. It was gone, and I remember thinking that was a big mistake.

LARRY FAULKNER *was a graduate student in chemistry.* President of UT-Austin from 1998 to 2006, he lives in Houston. It was like an injury that would never heal. And I instinctively felt that the way to get past that was to open the observation deck to the public again. I had that as a goal in my mind before I walked on campus as president, in 1998.

ANNIE HOLAND MILLER *was the student body president for the* 1998—1999 *academic year.* She lives in McAllen. The observation deck had been closed for so long that it had become a kind of mystical place. There were all sorts of folk tales around campus about the students who had jumped to their deaths, and Whitman, of course.

BOB HIGLEY: I love it when we're number one and they make it orange; that's a kick for me. But that's always at night, in the dark. During the day, if I see the Tower, I'm carried back. I think about how Paul Sonntag was eighteen years old when he died.

CLIF DRUMMOND: I'm a country boy, and so I had always loved to go to the Tower. It was a high place, and we don't have high places in West Texas. When you got up there, it was calm and cool, and you could see for a long ways. You could see all over campus, all over this beautiful city, way out to the Hill Country. People went up there all the time. And Charles Whitman ruined that. He took it away from us. It may sound trivial, but he took that away.

PAMELA COLLOFF is an executive editor at Texas Monthly, where she won a National Magazine Award in 2013. For "96 Minutes," she spent three months searching phone directories and driver's license records to locate and interview eyewitnesses of the Whitman shootings. This oral history was reprinted with permission from the August 2006 issue of *Texas Monthly*.

≫ UP IN THE WESTERN HILLS ≪

Written by **LAURA FURMAN** | **THE PUBLIC RADIO STATION** where I live in Austin broadcasts citizens' stories of when they first moved to town and, as I drive, I often listen in to the memories. There's the man who went to the lake for a swim, unknowingly taking a dip at Hippie Hollow, Austin's nude beach. There are young romances that turn into marriages of forty years' duration, and there are those people whose cars died when they were heading for California. No reason is too whimsical, too personal, too mundane. The stories are filled with affection and amusement. So small a thing brought them to the place where they're living out their lives.

The radio anecdotes of moving to Austin, and of staying, often stir a familiar feeling in me, an enjoyable sadness that the past trumps the present. It's a kind of nostalgia, *saudade, heimweh*. Homesickness, even in the place you call home. Call it whatever you like, it's an unfulfillable desire.

In the nostalgist's view, Austin used to be cheap, friendly, and populated by gentle, dope-smoking scholars and geniuses. They'll promise that if you turned up on any porch in the West Campus area near the University of Texas in the 1970s, you'd be sure of a bed, breakfast, maybe a whole new life, and all for free. This is the prevailing memory. What I call *It used to be* stories.

It used to be begins many Austin stories told when plenty of wine is drunk.

Here's one. It used to be that no building in Austin rose higher than the State Capitol, guaranteeing a clear view to the University Tower. When UT won a game, the Tower went orange and those in the legislature who were Longhorn fans could rest easy. Then a slick apartment building, the Westgate, was built by the side of the Capitol, just as tall as the pink granite structure.

This nostalgic point of view is that one has always missed the best of times, so when my husband and I moved to Austin in the early

1980s, we were of course too late.

When we moved, an expressway, MoPac, was already growing along the Missouri-Pacific right-of-way. All over downtown, nine-teenth- and early-twentieth-century buildings were being torn down to make way for architecturally undistinguished buildings. New developments were springing up to the north and south—even in the Hill Country.

When *Esquire* magazine called asking me to write about the Austin music scene, I wanted to write about Austin's growth. They weren't as interested as everyone here. But that's what everybody cared about. That's what everybody was talking about. How could we control growth? Was there a way to stop it? Or—why not let Austin expand?

I moved to Austin was in 1981 when I was awarded a writing fellowship, and lived on the Paisano Ranch just outside of Austin with my dog Blanche. The ranch was on a tumbledown road off another road. To get there I opened and locked two gates behind me and crossed Barton Creek. The ranch seemed like the backend of nowhere.

Down another farm to market road was the Salt Lick, a little stone building with a central barbecue pit and about ten tables. On rainy, cool winter afternoons, I sometimes met friends there. Between the stone and the light, we could have been in Italy.

On Memorial Day, there was a big storm and when the creek rose, we were trapped at the ranch. Once Barton Creek went back into its banks, I found out that the little grocery where I shopped, Whole Foods, had been devastated, along with car dealerships and Strait Music. Pianos were seen floating on Lamar. And at Whole Foods, the water had climbed halfway up the walls of the store. Customers pitched in with the cleanup, and there was a benefit to help the new grocery get back on its feet.

A year or so later, my husband and I moved to a rock house on nine acres in North Austin. The landscape was defined by limestone hills, canyons, scrubby oak trees, and tenacious cedar. A steep caliche drive led up to the house. Our landlord had made graveled paths and perennial beds defined by chunks of limestone. Lantana flowered, so did portulaca and loquat trees. Aside from pulling grass from the path and scooping live-oak leaves from the kidney-shaped pool that hung off the cliff, we had an easy time maintaining the grounds.

[*Downtown Austin*]

The house came with two chairs and a wooden trunk in which our landlord kept the possessions he didn't want to share. We didn't own all that much furniture or anything else, but the house looked fine half-empty. Next to us lived James and Lee in a trailer [when the weather was bad] but mostly outdoors in hammocks, beach chairs, and various rocks arranged around their fire-ring. Our dog Blanche loved being there as much as we did; she had the run of the woods and hills, except for the territory controlled by the neighboring cats.

We were beyond content in our commodious, easy corner of Austin until our landlord sold the property to a Dallas developer. We left the rock house and lived for the next decade in Lockhart, 29 miles south. Our neighbors James and Lee packed up their cats and moved to Elroy, near Bergstrom, the Air Force base.

One afternoon close to that time, I was having a cup of coffee at Manuel's on Congress Avenue with a friend talking about the changes. He was a Jane Jacobs developer with a psychic sense, and as he bemoaned the fact that you could find a parking space anywhere on Congress Avenue, he explained his vision of a busy, crowded, prosperous city. "This is the main street of *Texas*," he said, to prove his point.

I loved the wide open spaces on Congress. It made me think of my mother in New York, always moving our family car from one side of the street to the other. So the thought of sky-high hotels, citified shops, and national chains didn't sit well. It disrupted something in me. I wanted to protect places like Las Manitas, owned and run by two sisters, Cynthia and Lidia Perez. Their place was legendary. To get to the patio out back, you walked through the steaming, cheery, crowded kitchen where the delicious meals were made.

But my developer friend, he could see it. Years later, the building would be torn down to make way for a giant hotel, leaving us yearning for their vegetable tamales with mushroom sauce.

My father, until his last days, refused to divulge the name of the Ukrainian town that my grandfather left for America in the 1890s. My whole life, my father had always asked, "What difference does it make now?"

***

Today, I live across the river, up in the western hills, across many valleys from the rock house where we started. About fifty years ago, our neighborhood was built by people who wanted to live in the hills in a modest way. They mandated that no structure was to rise above tree line. The one-level homes that fit the rules of the professors, artists, and cedar-choppers who first settled here, now co-exist with multimillion-dollar half-rounds of glass and concrete, Tuscan villas, French châteaux, and Georgian mansions. In the early 1990s when we moved here we could see six houses across the valley, and now the number is doubled.

On a good day, at the right time, not at rush hour, not on 360, not on MoPac, it takes us about ten minutes to drive downtown to the movies or dinner out. In the same amount of time we're at the University. My favorite swimming holes are ten minutes away. My rowing center is about the same distance from home. Last July Fourth, my husband and I, and about a hundred other people, kayaked to a great spot between bridges to watch the fireworks flame up and away.

Friends have died since we moved Austin, including our dear landlord in the rock house. I miss them all. Some friends have moved away, while others have moved back. When you're in a very old city, like Rome, you can see and sense the layers of the past underneath the noisy present. I've been here long enough that my life in Austin is layered. I cherish the friends who remain and those who are gone, the places that used to be and the places that are.

One evening not long ago, I was driving up the hill at the start of our pretty road. It was the time when deer appear out of nowhere so I was going slowly, and slowed down more at a certain electric pole where sometimes a hawk sits to watch the sunset. All was familiar, all was calm, and I thought, *I live here, I live here.*

LAURA FURMAN is the author of three novels and four collections of short stories, and she is the series editor of *The O. Henry Prize Stories.* She is professor emeritus at the University of Texas at Austin.

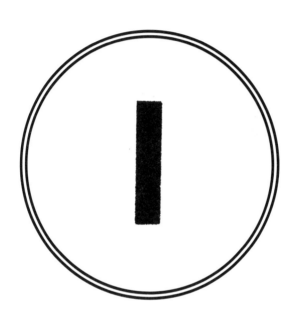

INDEX

⋙ INDEX ⋘

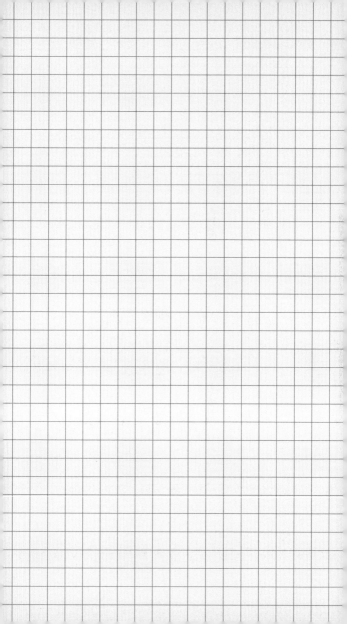

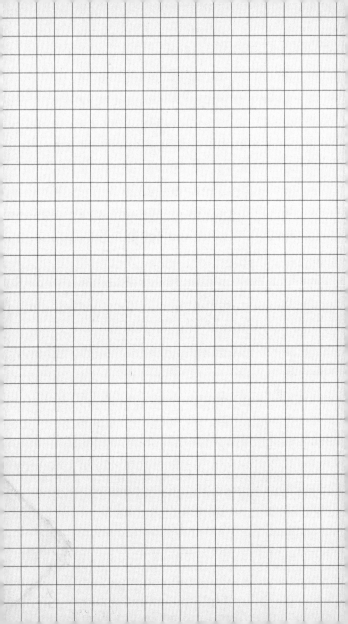